The Domino Effect

Book I – Narrow View Within My Circle

You can't sweep humans away.

Facebook.com/nohousenoless

The Domino Effect
Manifesto by Jackson

Book I – Narrow View
Within My Circle

Book II – A Wider View
Interviews and Investigation
Coming Winter 2017

Book III – Outcomes
The Good and Bad
Coming Fall 2018

ISBN: **0985560215**
ISBN-13: **978-0985560218**

Cover photography by MaxxsPhotography.com

Cover design by Jackson

DEDICATION

There are many ways that I could go in this dedication. In my last book the dedication highlighted many of the people that created turmoil in my life. Those individuals that drove the adversity into my life, which developed my writing as an outcome of their incongruent behaviors. Though enlightened entertainment to the reader and cathartic to my soul, this time I am going to award the dedication to those who had positive impact.

Joseph "JoJo" Martinez, as you read this know that my thoughts have been with you every day that I pen these words. You chose to have conversation with me and few others, I value every lesson that you have taught me about living on the streets. I love that you call me out when I am being stupid and oblivious to the reality of my street life. I also appreciate your constant oversight, keeping myself and others safe from harm every day and night, hope to **gallivant** again soon.

I only wish that on June 29th I had not drank enough to head back to camp before you. Not that it would have helped with these lawyers because they would not bother to put other witnesses on the stand. You got a bogus trial and were picked on because you were a Hill target. *I'm confident that the second you finish this chapter of this book you will be working on nothing other than a 2255 post conviction motion and getting a new trial for inadequate counsel.*

The joke is that the orchestration of that defense team was beyond good, but at the same time so absolutely incompetent. So, I am not able to blame the jury, only the stupidity of the defense. 1) Failing to point out the fact that there are 3 bars 50 yards before Union Station where anyone could have purchased her a drink or 5 if she in fact lost her debit card. When your mom and I both asked the lawyers separately to ask Grier that question on the stand and they refused: I could not have been more perplexed. 2) But also allowing the forensic toxicologist to testify that the DA asked her what the highest possible blood alcohol level could have been at 9 pm. What about the lowest possible, or even the average, but not a word about it from your defense team. The defense just allowed the expert to testify about what is the maximum drunk she could have been. 3) Not allowing Kellogg (who was totally available), or myself to testify was the icing, showing beyond any reasonable doubt they had already dealt the case away before even starting. To start the case from the jury questioning to your testimony mentioning Kellogg and then not calling him to the stand did nothing except represent that your statements could not be supported by your friends. He told me word for word what you testified, on the Hill in July in front of Max. I jumped up and down with excitement because he remembered the events so clearly down to the description of the girl. I said to him "if you turn out correct on her description there is no questioning you were present." 4) Failing to prep you as to their off the wall strategy of withholding your houseless status but not prepping you to not say camp on the stand is nuts. 5) To not inquire about or at least mention it in closing arguments, a woman carrying marijuana with her through the most well know weed park in the city, and not have any in her urine at all? She was bringing the candy to the tatted up stoners before she ever left the house. The Public Defenders offered a good defense if reviewing the transcripts, preventing any reasonable chance for overturning at appeal. They covered their asses but didn't realize I was paying attention to every word. And that I already knew this never happened as they claimed, you are not guilty of this charge period. I love you bro, Oi Oi.

Dustin, there is no way I would have spent the entire year of 2015 on the streets of Denver without you. Your gruff exterior and daily giggle kept me out there. You provided me a glimpse into a world of your street family that alone I would not have been privy. Our ability to be business partners as well was a bonus. Allowing me to contribute to your existence was a great blessing. Watching your growth was a reward.

You have no limits and I thank you for stretching my limits, long boarding trough Denver, sleeping in odd places, retiring to our riverfront camp! I enjoyed the good and ignored the turmoil, in hindsight you will always be a highlight of my early years in Denver. Thank you!

To my son Max thank you for so many of the pictures in the book and the cover shots. When you came to visit, and learned that I was a street dweller shortly before you arrived I didn't know how you were going to react. By the time you left town, you had the ability to look me in the eyes and say "I can see why at your age, with what you've done in life you would fall in love with this lifestyle."

Maxwell my oldest son who at 22 years old has once considered going into politics and perhaps someday becoming President of the United States. Max is always a straight shooter when addressing my quirks and odd behaviors. In this case me being a "homeless bum" as he had identified some of his brothers friends who had couch surfed at his college apartment was going to be an ear full, I told my street family not to be offended. When he arrived he also fell in love with the passive positive lifestyle, enjoying every minute of his vacation with me sleeping outside with us. Rather than me working or having to address a small business as in his previous time with me, he was able to explore with me and learn more about the street life. He and I both valued the care free, lazy days with little concern beyond his planned departure date. Now we spend hours on the phone just shooting the shit, whether school work or my daily walk outside we communicated well. When the events of October 2015 occurred, which was the catalyst for this manifesto coming to be, he offered insightful retort to my distress and anger. Thanx

Max

Anyang – Thanks for being my second. The only other person that takes time to listen without judgment. Offering sound love directed advise to me and our street family. Without your logic and ability to make others listen, my first year would have not been as successful.

Denver Park Ranger Eric Knopinski, thank you for your constant support with promotion of my Denver Urban Camping Ban alternative enforcement standards. I so much appreciate your input and recognition of my proposal delineating expectations of those living out doors. Thank you for your continued care for our parks here in Denver and the people that utilize them. You have been a contributor of knowledge and awareness in the lives of all the people you contact and helped me realize the publishing of this manifesto. And we know you have a job to do which sometime conflicts with our existence.

Thanks to every single person I have stacked on my hotel room floors, or that shared our camp at one point, you have all taught this old man new things daily. My street family that adopted me have been such an inspiring community that I choose this course for my writing! You all provide me support daily still.

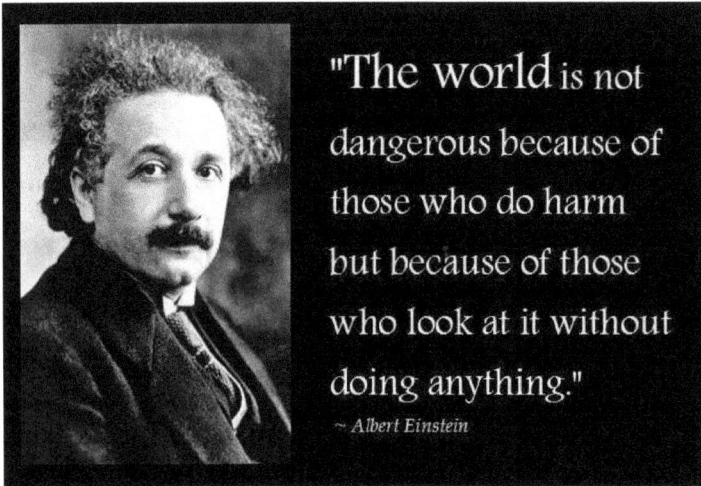

"The world is not dangerous because of those who do harm but because of those who look at it without doing anything."
~ Albert Einstein

Contents

15 Introduction

19 November 7, 2016

35 Shelter as Defined by Denver

45 This is my Dream for the Treatment

49 November 3, 2015

53 Thinking Out Loud

57 This is my Day Dream!

59 Start of FB Page

63 Words to live by!

65 Background/Unique Qualifications

77 Is there is Fate

81 More Thinking Out Loud

93 Entry Level Advancement/The Roots

103 Denver/Occupy 2012

   Urban Camping Ban Debacle

137 Housing Needs

151 Set Up For Failure Later

157 Hakuna Matata

171 Brand New Discoveries

179 Transients

187 The Smallest Percent

   Druggies / Slobs / Zero Respect

195 Background that Started This

201 Denver Picked On The Wrong

   Group

NOTES

POINTS

Agree	Disagree

Introduction

My current goals is to both to enlist the assistance of you the readers/advocates of these realities written herein, by providing my personal views, experience and support to a worthwhile group of individuals who lack a voice as well as a roof.

My investigation to date and the insight that has unfolded since that October evening have weighed heavily on my sprit. My freedoms of thought and movement have both been restricted; as well my equal right to protection under the same laws as my accuser, have been voided and dismissed as non-existent to the homeless of Denver.

On October 2, 2015, I found myself in a situation that seemed unfair, perverted and clearly bias on the part of my intransigent accuser, as well as the narrow mindedness of select Denver Police.

I have lived my life as an entrepreneur rarely finding myself in any situation requiring me to form a political perspective, needing voicing on any subject. Marijuana was the exception, its degree of illegality and damage done by the imposition of law and governance; versus the actual proof of damage done by the product itself was always a problem for me. Actually government drugs vs. weed as a whole, have been my prior outspoken dissatisfaction provided via government controls and law, but still only voiced among friends.

That was my previous major dissatisfaction with our political system. In this situation however, I find myself plucked from the free development of my life's direction and personal journey to shine a bit of light on a subject that is in the shadows too often, housing challenged Americans.

Through the last 3 months I am beginning to pen ideas to determine "if" what I am standing up for, is valid and logical, with substantive justification for focusing my energy, emotion and passion. It is and I have come to many profound realities and many logical conclusions that will unfold in the pages to follow.

And I have determined that not only does this topic earn my support, but I find a true lack of "Voice" in the segment of Americans who are in the greatest position of need. The segment with the greatest potential for improvement with proper support and guidance and training.

I commit whatever time and energy needed from this day forward to put an end to the inequality of Americans who are residentially challenged, those without a ROOF.

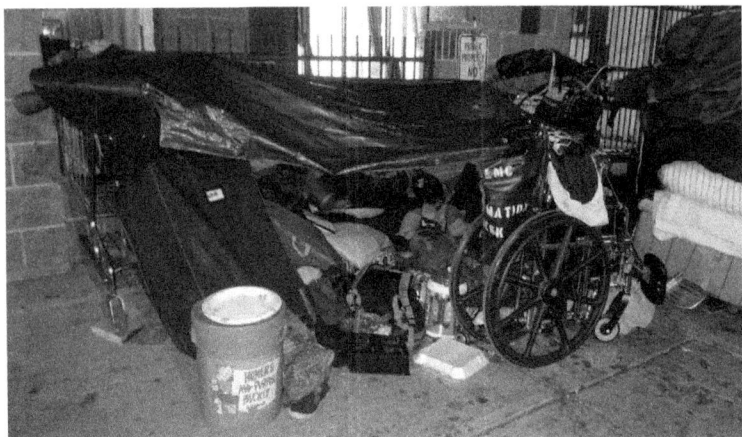

November 7, 2016
Thought of the Day

First week living back outside after 12 months indoors.

I can't sleep in my sleeping bag, I can get soaked or freeze because a tent that breaks down and travels with me is forbidden by imposition of law here in Denver, Colorado.

My street family and I, camp here for almost 3 years.

Judgments abound and are so less than accurate, highly assumptive and most time lacking empathy of any sort; mostly indignation and ridicule without interaction, investigation or cause. Solely judged by personal mores and pre-conceived notions of street people and why they exist.

If I am in need, I create, as I always have. Be it art or words, using my skills of hand and sharp mind no need is out of my reach, certainly not because of the lack of roof or walls. But I am aware I am the rare, stable business minded and trained individual that is retired from previous vocations and searching out my post 50 brainstorm idea that will sustain my next adventure and income stream. Income beyond my personal needs or desire, but matching my skill level as previous. Perhaps it would be nice to leave the excess to my 2 sons, yet I am pretty confident they will develop their own financial stability through entrepreneurship and providing amazing service in whatever they choose. Each earning monetary stability at a level they desire, not demanded or implied by social norms or inheritance.

A Solid Roof I am told is required to establish home. To this I must disagree, it seem to me the largest lie ever sold. Marijuana causes "Reefer Madness" 1937 film doesn't even compare as total government (institutional) programmed lies go.

The roof I once owned gave me great pride in "home". The roof I once owned was surrounded by 4 walls with views through rectangle vacancy in brick and mortar; filled with glass that needed to constantly be cleaned to the reveal the visible sliver of the world within view. My home for 20 years or so was not by any means my house or that of my parents; it was where my heart was from the age of 20 until 40 just a decade ago. It was Echo Pizza in Voorhees New

Jersey, the business I began from the ground up with my initial, blood, sweat and lack of sleep. After the first year, I was aided from many others who shared passion for my vision and business goals, whom I developed into a higher thinking employees. Most were teens and this was their first or second job, ever. Those that lasted past the first week, where given skills that carried through in everything they do even 30 years later. I know this because I am reminded by so many of my former staff often thanks to the connection of social media.

I felt I was in my true home, because of the business, the staff, the town, the community not the walls and roof. The first year before profit, I dwelled inside the office of the store and had no shower or bed yet I did have a roof, walls and the biggest kitchen I could ever dream of. I slept on the pizza bags covered with a sheet, ate only pizza which cost me almost nothing, and bathed at Bally's Total Fitness a block away.

I lived indoors in a beautiful house growing up as well as having my own apartment from 18 to the day I signed a $2000 a month triple net lease. Homeless with little thought at 20, a fact hidden from my parents due to my embarrassment. I knew working 18 hours a day to start would be just right for my plans. What would be the point of a bed and shower using store generated capital to pay for a second roof, elsewhere. It is illegal to reside in a commercial business in Voorhees, yet no thought of consequence ever entered my entrepreneurial mind; just that $600 a month being diverted on my P & L for a second roof a second bathroom, a second lamer kitchen, plus bed, $600 to better invest in advertising and marketing.

I was born in Brooklyn NY in 1966 to Helen and Sonny, I was always instilled with the idea there were no limits holding me down from making anything I desires occur. By the young age of 20 I was 150 miles from my New York home and family. I landed myself just outside Philadelphia to find the fulfillment of the pizza dream.

My avenue of creating cash was manifested by my heart, head and hands, along with the burning desire and written goals which constantly evolved but always centered on Echo's improvement. My skills were refined, my talents were very clear. Sales reached high six figures annually by year three. Eventually expanding into 4200 sq ft with seating for 150 and a Ben and Jerry's Ice Cream Shoppe inside my store. There was never a need to brag or discuss revenue it was in clear view of all.

My dad purchased and maintained a house from age 35 in 1972 until his death in 2013. Great investment as life goes, 40k to 400k in just under 40 years. This dream was his, not mine! He did it all, he did it right and he died speaking the words "I'm stubborn. I gotta do it my way." I could not agree more.

His way, a 5 AM start of the day and a 4:30 return home time daily Monday thru Friday for almost 30 years. He knew the grind would provide his American Dream: stability for my mom, 4 year elder sister and myself, period. He got a good Union job delivering Yodels, Ring Dings, Devil Dogs and Funny Bones for Drake's Cakes in NYC. Delivering to bodegas, local shops and large markets. Earned his wage and stole through what the drivers termed tips, to live his life his way, which was slightly above his actual means for many of the years of his employ. He supported a stay at home mom, my sister and me throughout.

My father spent time in all of the 5 boro's of New York City, Staten Island was the only place he did not live growing up. He started life in the Harlem projects then the Bronx, then Brooklyn followed by Queens where his parents finally settled down in a small single story house with 2 bedrooms and an attic. My granddad ran numbers out of his dry cleaners.

When my dad married his crush and my mom married her hero, they moved into Trump Village in

Brooklyn. I lived in this built to be affordable 2 bedroom apartment with my sister and I sharing a bedroom with bunk beds.

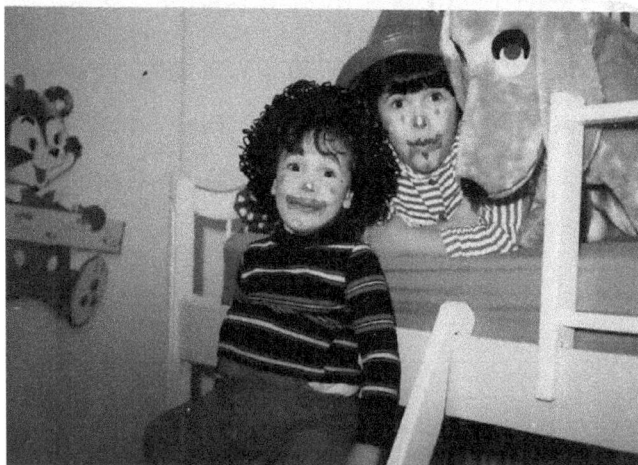

Today a brother and sister must have separate bedrooms in many cities. Why? The apartment building I lived in until age 4, I remember as a high rise maybe 30 plus floors, and the units were 3 times larger than needed in this situation of abundant unhoused Americans.

Eric on drums at Trump Village, Brooklyn NY 1968

Dad had his side hobbies, which keep me occupied and out of trouble, he chose his passion allowing me to be included every weekend for 5 years. Obviously I jumped at the chance. I observed that his part time hobby, on weekends generated more money in less time than the vocation he choose for secure income.

Baseball Collectibles, specifically in the 80's when cards still had high value, Sonny Jackson was a large presence in the hobby and for certain the profits followed. He was also a shrewd businessman which at that time I discovered by watching and learning. As much as I tried, he would not insert himself full time in a world he loved and was proven profitable for him. He could have been his own master, in my mind, instead of slaving and complaining about work related stresses weekly, within the house, in my ear shot. Though not talking with me, I was forever impacted by the stress from dads various supervisors. I only perceived dad as a slave to the paycheck, pension, and benefits for both life and death.

This was totally right minded thinking for my Dad because his goal was his. In his death he had no regrets short of not using the words "I Love You" as much as he felt it. I told him he was wrong to regret

28

that, because in every breath he took my sister and I both knew at all times we were loved tremendously by him, even though the words were absent. Because that was who Dad was, "talk's cheap, show it".

Back to me, and the so many like minded folks under 50, survival is our key to making dreams come true. Finding the road to our dreams often takes wandering around. Some, like myself get lucky for skill and well managed passion the first time out. Others take lots of searching and trying to find their hobby that will yield finance and financial long term stability along with happy fulfillment.

My kids mom once expressed to my eldest son, "Not all who wander, are lost." I agree.

In my opinion many younger people are seeking their niche in life, which foremost provides enjoyment as well as sufficient income. This desire for happiness within a career is new. A very different priority versus our fathers and grandfather thinking. The world is very different and to ignore the changes and flaws, just applying for jobs based on pay not enjoyment and happiness, doesn't work for many of us. To think like that is completely absurd to those who think like me, we want work that we can enjoy. The concept of it's a job and it doesn't matter if you like it or not, is not us!

For the first time since 14 years old, I am wandering without a road map and timeline requirements for arrival at my written goals. Beyond Denver as the location, I remain undetermined for the last three years, and comfortable I will find my passion and finance will attach to it. I have started to develop some new income streams in the past few weeks so it is clear to me I am doing what's right for me. I also love my new hobby of growing legal marijuana in my closet when I was indoors 12 months of the 2 plus years here. Growing weed is a career with potential that appeals to me in some ways, and here in Denver there are many opportunity in that market, but I have not committed to anything, yet. My uncertainty should not be for anyone or any government to judge or prevent me from hunting down my next desire, while loafing without a roof.

I have no house, no roof, but I sure am at home in downtown Denver. My house is in one of my bags, because regardless of negatively impacting law in Denver, I will protect myself from the lethal elements of this winter in my Kelty tent.

No doubt for me, my two plus years here, now on the street more than half the time with no roof beyond nylon, I am happier outside than in a mortgaged or rented roof with walls. Why?

I often ask myself the same question.

My first answer is living out of doors offers a much different view of the everyday valued items in your own little world. Sustained by your own will and aided by protection from those who immediately surround you when sleeping, each and all protecting each other's personal property.

Property is no different a Right in a house, shed or strapped to a bicycle cart, regardless it is protected by identical law. Yet owned or collected personal property of a person without a roof, regardless of reason is treated as refuse.

Throughout the City, Denver police, City workers and some contracted, and occasionally yet considerably less the Parks and Rec will at arbitrary whim, define items as abandoned or trash and destroy or dispose of a person's select few items that the owner finds valuable enough to carry and hold onto. Perhaps during a coffee break or bathroom run, being public facilities are few and far between, property abandoned momentarily but surely returned for rapidly is ceased. I have observed this rapid return amid their items being tossed in a refuse truck.

This happens often in Denver and it makes me sick to see or hear when it does take place.

Denver is too forward thinking positive a community to not figure out a better way to address street dwellers that are outside by choice and better assist those stuck outside against their will, due to one or two lacking items needed to get themselves back safely indoors. In the latter case if one chooses to sleep for a month in their car or behind a dumpster or on a subway grate, they should not have their world obliterated further by police intervention or costly tickets for being without a roof. This behavior from government, making laws which in fact criminalize house absent folks, preventing individual control, progression of self and freedom to pursue their direction as they see fit, is not helpful.

Further detriment inflicted upon anyone who is living outside, who may have hopes of next week being the time they can get a place and things back in order for their life goals, is beyond cruel, lacking forethought from the perspectives of those displaced, and our cultural intelligence.

For those wishing to explore and wander, why is that a great boast worthy thing for an American to backpack through Europe, with almost no income potential. But try backpacking as an American in America, I will bet you encounter more police than enrichment, which is everywhere around all of us if not disrupted by absurd laws and instilling of fear by officials.

Written in my tent on the Platt River in a three hour longhand rant. At least half of this book is derived from spontaneous writing beginning but not ending with the dog poo incident in October of 2015.

Shelter as Defined by Denver

I first arrived in Denver and choose to sleep outside rather than pay for a hotel room in June of 2014. I did this Downtown illegally for 2 of the 4 weeks I visited Colorado. I flew in from Philly and was planning on learning about the area for the entire month. Max my oldest and his cousin Steph were going to pick me up sometime in the second week. I spent about 12 days roaming around southern Colorado with the two of them. He dropped me off back in Denver for me to spend the last few days. I flew from Denver to Florida to visit Jake my younger son at the end of my Denver stay. June 2014 for me was the first time in my life I had ever slept outside.

Back to the indoors, about 2 weeks in Florida then back to Manhattan for the first all nude body paint day. Then I returned to New Jersey where I spent about a month tying up loose ends before moving back to Denver for my foreseeable future. I lived the first month with one of the people I met my first time through in a downtown high-rise. And never really liked sleeping indoors anymore. I spent up to 18 hours hanging out at Stoner Hill downtown. Writing and enjoying the vibration that the other stoners from round the world and all over the United States. I continued living indoors with few bills and 100% free time to do as I pleased, which I spent almost all of at the Hill in Commons Park. I felt a connection to the type of people that were here at the Hill the first minutes and they were almost all stoners. There were plenty that used other drugs but not when they were at the Hill. It was an amazing and constant anthropology and sociology lesson. I figured anyone could put together a high quality thesis paper for their doctorate on the Hill dwellers without any problem, because of how diverse and mixed origin these folks are.

Problems began within the first days of my moving from a downtown apartment to the streets again using the tent and sleeping bag I had bought for my June trip, this time I also had my car with me.

Parking tickets and 2 hour metered parking, both cost me about a grand over the first 2 months before I sold the car to stop the cycle. Many people would have just slept in the car but for me that was out of the question. I have never been able to get any sleep in anything where I cannot stretch out my body completely. So I set my tent up outside by the local day service provider, where everyone else had been sleeping. This was in contrast to when I slept down by the river alone, when I spent time in June. The Parks Dept had come in and cut back all the brush that concealed my tent and many others. As well as eliminating any areas near the Hill for people to do other drugs out of sight which was the one positive. So I choose to join the rest of the people that slept outside a local homeless collation building. The first time I was disturbed by the police for being in my tent on the side of a city street I was asked to take it down I found that to be totally reasonable at around 6am.

The following nights I choose not to use the tent at all and instead to sleep on the sidewalk in just the sleeping bag. I was much more prepared to live on the streets than most. It's often the ability to acquire and retain the proper gear that enables success on the streets. Aside from the car for storage those first months in front of the collation I always have abided the rule, the right tools for the job . In this case all the camping gear need to survive weather and whatever eventually came. Meanwhile others were just on the sidewalk with blankets over them and maybe a cuddle buddy to share it with. Keeping in mind this was the middle of August, the temperature was not any big deal.

The next time I was woken by Denver police it I was told that I was not allowed to have erected a shelter on the street. I could not understand what the officer was saying to me. I did not have my tent up; I was just laying on the sidewalk with just the sleeping bag. He went on to let me know that here in Denver any time you have something above and below you, you become guilty of erecting a shelter on city property. I again really could not follow as you may be having trouble with right now, following Denver's meaning of shelter.

Shelter in Denver Colorado is in fact any time a person has something underneath them while at the same time having something over them. So for instance in this case if I were sleeping on top of the sleeping bag, it would have been just fine, or if I was on the concrete sidewalk with the sleeping bag over me I would also be just fine. But because I was between the layers I had erected a shelter according to the letter of the law in Denver. Now clearly this is not the reality, a shelter offers some level of permanent affixing to the location where it rests. Imagine the tornado sirens going off and jumping in a sleeping bag to complete the request of seek shelter immediately! It's such a joke. But as shown in a chart later in these pages, only 17 camping tickets were issued over 4 years, so no one has ever stuck to not guilty, long enough in court to test the stupidity of the law, and the definition of shelter therein.

I have now been warned that in the park shelter tickets will be issued if my tent is seen by Rangers. The same tent I have been seen using for a few years now, here in the same area with the same Rangers. They are now getting pressure from above, to follow the letter of the law, no matter how absurd.

I asked if my rain fly above me and no tent under me would be a satisfactory sun and wind block. I was told yes, so long as long as I am sitting on the grass or dirt not a blanket or tarp. I wonder how, if I am sitting in a chair and my butt is protected from the dirt it is in fact erecting a shelter? It would be funny if it were not so truly sad.

To redefine shelter for the sake of harming and criminalizing those on the street struggling is absurd. I am not claiming to be in the struggling position, I am just a 50 yr old man well aware of the spiders, rats and other wildlife that avoid my tent while crawling into or over blankets and sleeping bags of others. I think I need to fashion a tent that is topless. One that will have walls and a floor just not a roof and be within requirements when I sit here during the day working and keep the tent up as an office and vague separation from the outside. Even if the tent is open it is a structure because there is a top and bottom. There is no good reason I should have to scheme to sit in an open tent in the park to type on my laptop or write with somewhat independent space. And to use this standard for rain and snow, ice and hail seems a bit reckless to the human being. Someone can freeze on the sidewalk with many blankets over them just nothing on the concrete. A small tent to block wet and wind that breaks down and folds up to carry away upon request when the inclement weather subsides is a life saver, period. It changes the temperature and the wind and the water saturation, which are all life threatening in Denver winters. These cases of frostbite and death are things that should never happen because an unhoused person is in fear of jail able offenses over their own safety.

There was an old standard that officers and officials could not disrupt the free choice of the course of someone's day unless they were apparently about to commit a crime. Crime requiring Mens Rea, the intentional forethought of being criminal, as a state of mind. The simple act of being tired and finding proper shelter being beyond your ability at that moment is criminal; how? Sleeping safely is just common sense and takes a level of responsibility to keep hold of tents and sleeping bags. To say a person is criminal for this behavior is one of the saddest evolutions our Country has derived as a problem solver of the houseless; and their greater financial dilemmas caused by others more often than laziness or irresponsibility of the person needing such protection to keep safe from deadly weather or diseased critters.

These are the simple things that can be corrected by a standard of treatment of Americans without housing. I pray as I pen these words that someone of influence takes this as a serious issue on a National level as well as here in Denver. If any of the corrections in this book are able to be implemented there will be a complete shift to housing all Americans and providing safety and respect to those currently living on the streets.

Update post proof – Supervisor Ranger told me for the park ordinance that a "structure" consists of a roof and a floor. So if you wrap yourself tarp creating a roof and a floor you are in violation of park regulations. So I did it, I cut the roof off my tent, and when he saw me next, I was not violating the law.

Cut the roof out of my tent! No structure here!

This is my Dream for the Treatment of Americans lacking permanent addresses!

Elimination of a manufactured *word* from the all electronic and paper documents ASAP and questioning via any interview process. In order to affect change we the People of this established Nation must immediately strike at the heart of the problem. Elimination of any attempt to usurp Individual Rights, through imposition of law to protect, as well repeal of current laws which further undermine struggling Americans.

Similar to "don't ask, don't tell" the official United States Military Codes regarding an individual's Right to freely pursue their own human development regarding sexuality. Decades of disrespect to American members of our Military came to an end, because of the recognition that sexuality choices did not redefine the character of the individual and was by no means criminal within the ranks.

When I am addressed by a person that has a permanent address, and any part of their statement includes the word "homeless" it most always seems to carry the same indignant tone as any supremacist using "nigger" in their vernacular. More often than not it is very degrading to my humanity, and condescending to my choice of existence.

First and foremost stop describing the lack, by the addition of the suffix "less" to a deeply emotionally rooted word Home. I challenge you to think of three American words that contain "less" as a suffix, which cannot be scaled as a negatively polarized compound word.

Federal goals and housed Americans that attempt to rectify the situation of Americans displaced from permanent residence are very diligent yet still fail to correct the root issues, start with improvement of the all defining use of language. It will change the dynamic of any related conversations.

46

Secondly, provide protection from hate crimes by adding the group "no permanent residence". Federal hate crime measures in my opinion should be amended to include a line within the defined categories reading "or as a court determines the actors' initiation of criminal offences to be based on bias as the preponderance of reason for such actions."

November 3, 2015

It has come to my attention, for reasons I can only explain as mind bending, in cities throughout America including my City of Denver, homeless people have become crime targets.

Why?

Many would think they have little to take or envy, so who would commit a crime against a homeless person. Most people will never really understand because they have humanity that overpowers greed, fear and hate. Yet, those with fear and disdain who seemingly ignore the homeless and those who aggressively degrade the homeless have perpetuated and manifested a stigma that homelessness itself is the crime.

Crimes perpetrated against homeless individuals yields no need for punishment, because homeless folks are already criminals and less American than the remainder of those living in houses, protected under the laws.

Often the criminal behavior comes from a fed up resident or residents of high priced surrounding homes and businesses; feeling negative affected of the presence of groups they defined homeless, congregating in areas local to themselves. The old *"I didn't mean for it to go that far, but someone had to do something to get them out of here."*

Many housed people agree with lawbreaking tactics, and some that don't agree still somehow justify and condone the housed lawbreaker vs. the oppressed homeless individual, based on financial status alone. As with most oppression we have seen in America's history, crime against the lesser is not crime at all **in the eyes of the bigot.**

Taking the previous paragraphs into deep consideration I have concluded that the homeless

50

population in the entire United States have been classified by average Americans as "Less Than" therefore creating an acceptance of unfair treatment and ridicule.

Thus any individual choosing to cause harm or damage to an individual due to their homelessness, their socio-economic classification, those actions if criminal should be treated as "hate crimes" as defined by the law of the governing states or federal mandate.

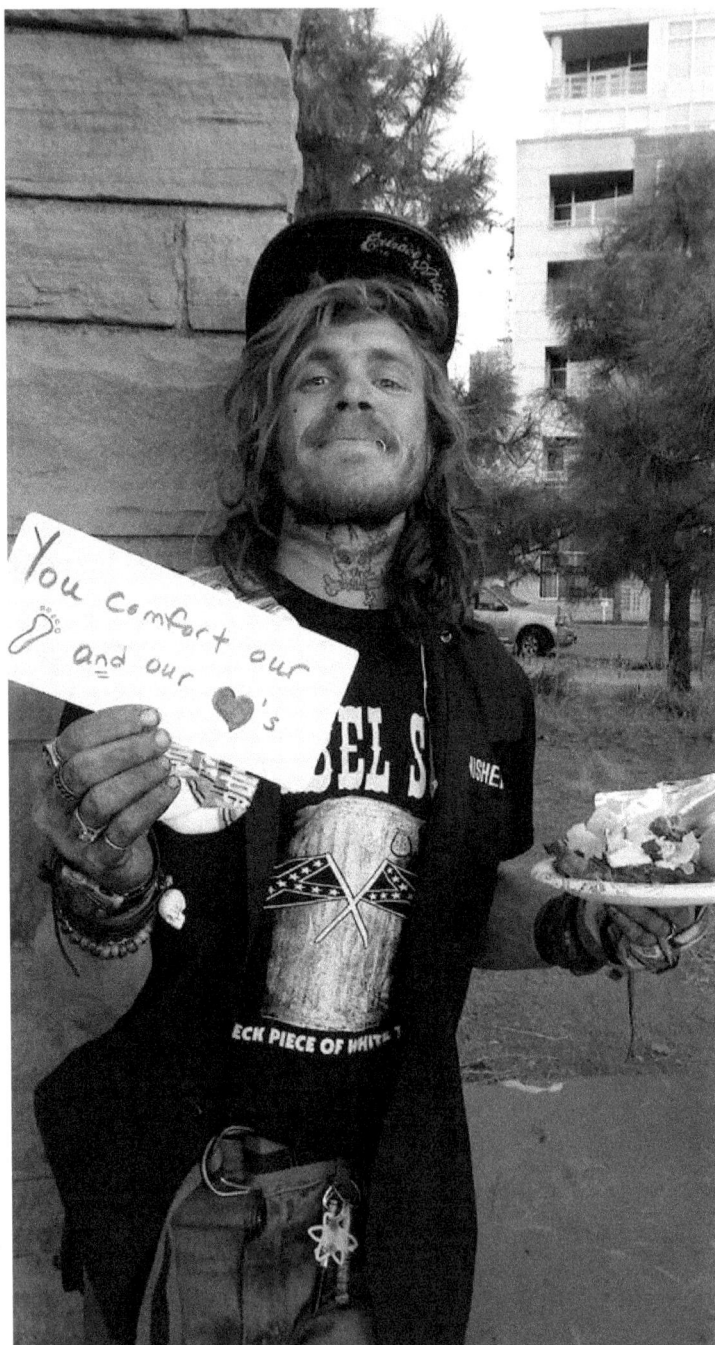

Thinking Out Loud

Home-less : the new 4 letter word in my mind

If ~~retarded~~ the "R" word is no longer PC
Even though the word retarded means "slow"

It is time for Americans to stop using the word home-less. Home is a place of belonging and warm personal connection

"Home Is Where The Heart Is"

The above expression predates the word homeless Home-less is degrading among those who remain feeling at home in their community although residentially challenged, whether short or long term displacement be their situation

Let us consider no longer addressing the many diverse individuals and communities of residentially challenged Americans into this automatically degrading all encompassing title

She looks at home to me every morning!

To me it falls into the Pygmalion category, the Rosenthal–Jacobson study telling students in Group 1 that they were smarter and gifted while Group 2 was treated to remedial work

It was quickly proven that Group 1 excelled only because of the title gifted/smarter, while Group 2 worked down to the expectations and showed faltering behaviors

So let us consider in our current state of American understanding of degrading titles continually redirecting what is PC and or polite

It is time to change the box from "homeless" to <u>"no permanent residence (long term/short term)"</u> and allow the individual to circle which reflects their goal A wealth of information would be measureable based on the two choices of long term or short term

If an American, residentially challenged applies for aid and circles short term, different options may be applicable

As well, stronger support networks can be established for those who believe they face long term lack of permanent residence

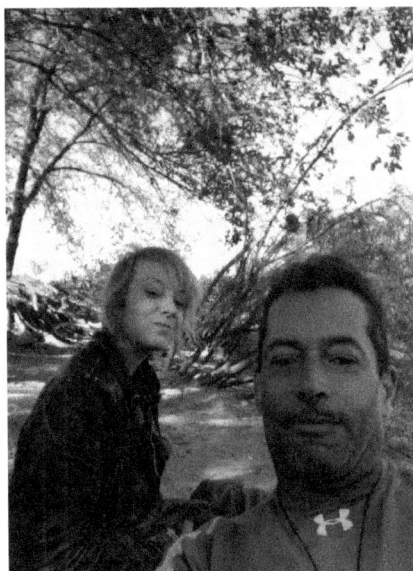

This is my Day Dream!

First and foremost stop describing "the lack" and get rid of the word homeless, to the more accurate *houseless*, which provides only a 2 letter change in most documentation and legislature.

Federal goals and Housed Americans that attempt to rectify the situation of Americans displaced from permanent residence, start with improvement of the all defining term. It will change the dynamic of any related conversations.

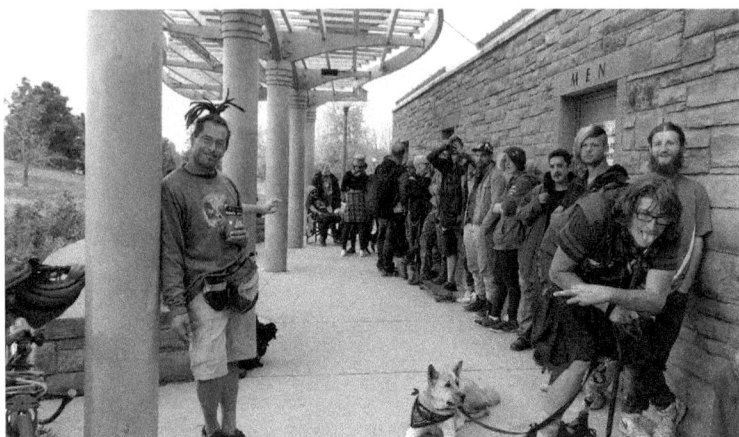

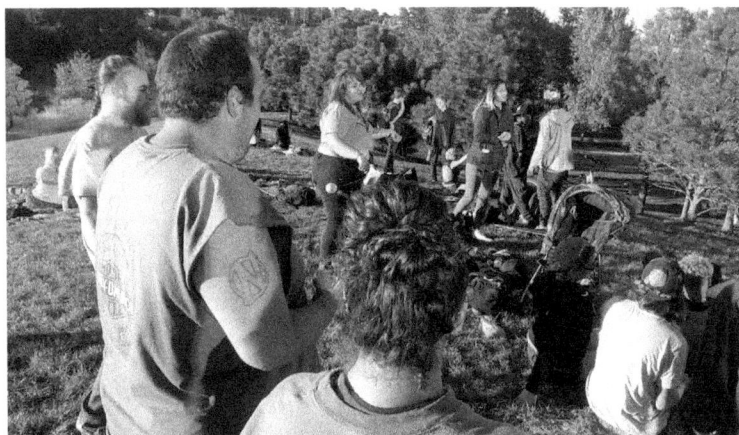

Start of FB Page

My Facebook page and hash tag are very easy to remember and tell others without the need of a pen or device, #nohousenoless will also be the official hash tag of my newly inspired manifesto. I pray with my friends and newcomers here, that the ideas within this FB page will plant a seed.

Americans lacking housing need to take back control of their identity, no longer be labeled as less than house owners, renters, and dependents of the like.

I've met and talked with many young people that have been moved from their birthplace or childhood residence and feel completely homesick because parents divorce or otherwise relocate too long a distance to visit regularly; the place where the youth truly considers HOME. I never asked this, yet I know they were not missing the Bricks and Sticks of their residence, they missed their personal support system of individuals and interaction with their former community at large.

I have to thank Doug W White for his attempt to jail me for his own criminal behaviors, big fail on his part, yet the 4 months waiting on the court's entry, that his charges were being dismissed against me, many things brand new to my awareness became very spotlighted.

As our Declaration of Independence commands, if you recognize a repeated injustice being perpetrated against a group, and have the ability to impact that with positive change, as an American you are obligated to do so.

All Movements begin with ONE VOICE, being a Barry Manilow fan, I know that one voice by virtue of singing a loving tune becomes many voices. Voices that can affect change.

I by no means am attempting to correct the larger issues within government, society, and social support systems causing there to be millions of un-housed American born individuals being vilified and criminalized by their neighbors in a growing number of American Cities. My goal is singular in this message. Eliminate the USE OF THE WORD! It is cruel because the all defining word has developed into a classification by those seeking power over others, houselessness is curable, often temporary situation, causing anguish and long term esteem issues in those being dehumanized. Now with criminalization of feeding and helping those on the streets, it is becoming illegal to get sleep in many major cities in America.

I always thought a catnap in the park on a beautiful afternoon was recommended for long life!

Thank You
Jackson
Feb 16, 2016

--*Update Jan 31, 2017* - *One year later and the constant thoughts mulling through my mind and various other events have caused me to change the goal, from just correction of the terminology assigned to those displace from a solid roof - to offering answers and comprehensive solutions to most facet's (60%+) of the growing populous of Americans living on the streets, also touching on camping/backpacking in America.*

Words to live by!

In life we are given two choices.

To be governed by Love or by Fear.

Love sees greatness in all things.

Fear discriminates and separates always!

Love allows us to enjoy the now!

Fear causes us to live in the past,

and clouds the present.

Love allows us to express ourselves openly.

Love allows pain to subside

With love things never need to see an end,

only a new direction to travel.

Without Love we are not allowing ourselves our

humanity!

Eric Jackson 5/2/1992 ©

Background/
Unique Qualifications

Coney Island - Trump Village 1970's Photo by: Musik Animal

I was born Eric Todd Jackson of Brooklyn New York in 1966. My father, the wise man that he was, in the late 60's, had only one thought: "What's best for the kids?" So as soon as possible he moved my mom, sister and me from Trump Village to the growing rural area of Long Island New York to a town called Lake Ronkonkoma.

I attended Sachem High School where I excelled in science and mathematics.

My scholastic goals were to become a Chiropractor back in the 80's before any understanding of the art was truly accepted by modern medicine of the day. Though, everyone else told me to be a lawyer. Life ran its course and I became a product of the business environment that I grew up in. Thank you Mark Lewis and Dad!

At forty-five years old I began imagining myself going to school for something that causes me to major in the sciences. The thing is I know, "it is never too late with structured goals."

I reflect back to the elementary school only being an average student yet getting 100% plus all the extra credit answers in my science classes. It was so unusual for me that two of the "smart kids" in my class accused me of cheating on a 6th grade exam. My teacher Mr. Maier trusted that I had not cheated yet asked me if I would take the test again with new questions on the exact same topic. I gladly wished to prove my innocence. I took the test alone in a study area of Wenonah Elementary School. Once again I aced the test. Mr. Maier was so proud he came into the classroom and admonished my wrongful accusers by announcing to the entire class while specifically addressing Steven and Jeffery; "By the way, he not only got a score of 104 again, but he spelled the same words wrong." Eugene Maier built confidence within me that day. I carry that support with me in my daily walk.   He may have been aware of what he did for my confidence, but for me the understanding only came in my business ownership years, making sure that anyone that contributed to our success got public credit for their commitment.

When I hit my 8th grade year in Junior High School the same would apply. I received great grades in math and science. One story I recall in science class stands out to me. I spent the entire first week with my head down on the desk and my eyes closed. That Friday the third day of school the teacher gave us a quiz on the classroom work he had covered the two days previous. I aced it. The comment Monday when I put my head down while he handed back the quizzes was, "Jackson, I don't know what you think you are doing, but it is not going to go on in my classroom!" After class I approached him politely and explained "sometimes for me, hearing something with my eyes closed allows it to sink in my head much better." Letting him know the manner in which I was able to learn best made my argument successful. He never gave me any friction in his class for the remainder of the year.

When I hit Sachem High School students moved into elective classes. I consistently choose the math and sciences to load my elective credits. The only English elective I opted for was Mr. Fabian's Intro to Publishing class; that was the year that my dad and I were publishing THE TRADER SPEAKS a monthly baseball card and memorabilia magazine. I wanted to learn the technical aspects of the newspaper and magazine publishing trades, never realizing that some of those lessons would be guiding me today, as

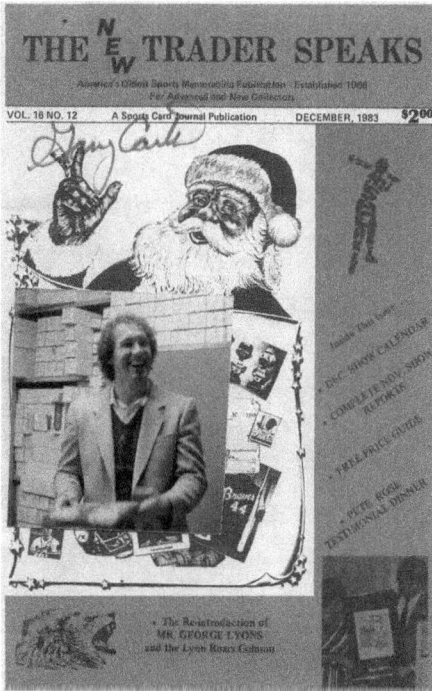

I sit here developing this manifesto. The purchase, publishing and subsequent sale to SCD, the still largest memorabilia niche publisher, taught me more lessons than I can count. First, my dad trusted my ideas as not just crazy and farfetched and secondly that I would always be able to depend on his support, plus so much about publishing.

This lesson of supporting me, allowed me a couple of years later to plan and execute the first baseball card collector show with more than a few professionals signing autographs as a pull for attendees, allowing dealers to encounter additional audience. My concept was considered crazy by industry leaders, yet my dad pulled out all the stops and assisted me both financially and with his time and efforts to accomplish my goal. And June 23 of 1985 I landed myself in the sports section of USA Today for Expo 85 Reunion of the 69 Mets. That was at 18 years old.

Downtown Athletic Club, New York City, me center, dad far left.

Two years later I opened a pizza business in Southern New Jersey after discontent working for Domino's and constant supervisor turnover. Starting my own pizza place seemed the logical step to me, yet now at

50 I realize it would not be the logical step to most other people.

I am graced with the awareness that I can personally achieve any goal I set for myself. Goals have been my keel, steadying my focus and direction in life. These goals are constructed by me and approved the moment they hit paper. Not every one has come to fruition, nor are those achieved always in the timeline prescribed on paper, but it works and I know it works. I have made this same process work for others, which further encodes the utility of why written goals connect directly to achievement in my brain.

Echo Pizza and several others businesses sustained myself and family for many years. At 25 I married young enough to father a baseball team of children, and it was amazing for 7 years. Only two boys from the marriage now 23 and 24; and I would have the other 7 today if I had the "gold" and a quality candidate for a mother to support such a decision.

Yet having more children is no longer a priority in my thoughts as when the goal was written in 1990.

My sons max and Jake at 3 and 4 in my back yard.

Yes, marriage and children were a written goal of mine, not just an accident or afterthought of sexual relationships.

I maintained my virginity until 18 and even then reluctant to spoil my goal of saving penetration for marriage. But in that case my girlfriend and hormones overpowered the goal. Perhaps that was the point I realized passion was inherent in my thinking and the passion came via my goals, but mixing love emotions with a goal is even better than passion alone. Most all of my goals were directed toward achieving what I loved and passion came along with it. Now looking back, my notebooks tone did change from things and property goals to lifestyle and associations around 18 so failing my goal and losing my virginity may have been pivotal in retrospect (as I write and reflect I am including conclusions in the writing for my own record).

Divorced in 1998 and still keeping to my goals I stuck around New Jersey, contrary to advice of others including my dad, to run away, I stayed for both my kids and the solid foundation of my business. The thoughts of starting over elsewhere were attractive and appealing to me who welcomes change, but there was no way in my reality to put distance between me and my kids, so love once again trumps goals based on desire. Had I written down move blah blah miles away and start a business doing blah blah, I would have been able to achieve the goal. I may have missed out on many valuable lessons in life had I separated from them and my New Jersey Home at that point in life. Perhaps preventing me from sitting here in Colorado typing these words. (upon proof reading this book, Max thanked me for staying put in New Jersey and not leaving before they did.) ☺☺

Being a businessman and <u>minimum wage employer</u> most of my life, opens my eyes of many of the issues of houseless individuals in America. Also why the title of this manifesto is The Domino Effect, because of my recognition that each and every challenge in the lives of those living on the streets were on top of the last challenges.

These adversities continue to pile up because of the current structure of our governing bodies. Core issues must be addressed as a whole to include fee and fine exemptions for financial hardship utilizing community service instead. The compiling costs of various things that a higher income worker just writes the check, without thought that it was going to cause the rent to be late or a car payment. These causal items are threaded throughout this document and there are many concisely demonstrating the overall domino effect on the lower income earners of America. Suspension of a person's drivers license because they are late on child support, adding fees for re-instatement of the driving privileges is beneficial to whom? Certainly not the child of the now law breaking parent, unable to pay for the child or go to work legally, if they drive.

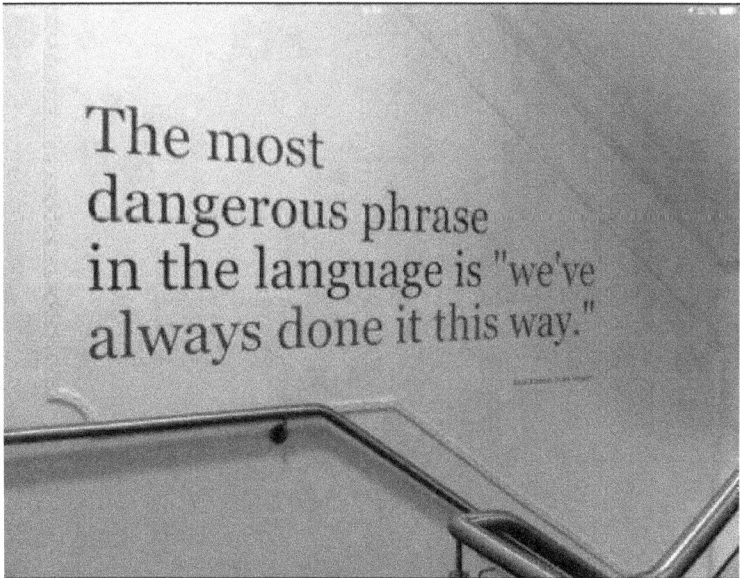

The most dangerous phrase in the language is "we've always done it this way."

Average population of Stoners at the Hill

Ranger Hill and I chatting at the Hill

Is There is Fate?

There are moments in time when an individual comes through enough that they realize their hypothesis is THE ANSWER, even if they were not searching for it.

It is something every person experiences at various points of their lives; but only select few are in tune with their own absolute correctness, until after someone else takes action on the idea. You will recall hearing "I invented that years ago!" yet they took no action to bring the invention of their minds-eye into reality. Those who take action and put fire underneath themselves, and with those actions create the next great thing.

I have consistently looked in the mirror mid-theory and building the complete thought, knowing beyond my cockiness, I've got it! "It" being the most accurate hypothesis and therefore correct and implementable plan to create or fix whatever.

When I dreamed up the 69 Mets reunion, I knew I had the outcome written in my notebook, which would play out exactly as written and be a slam dunk success. The same applied to most of the businesses I've founded and run, unless greed directed.

I am viewing this manifesto's publishing like it has already taken place. Manifesting the concepts I have dreamed up and wrote down.

Dating back to the second grade I was described as "the only one". The only one that thinks like that. While others would attempt some level of people pleasing thus fitting in better, hearing that, not me! I never gave a second thought, no matter how often it was pointed out how differently my thinking was.

My Grandma Ada brought three things into my world which I am now sure gave me unusual perspectives of the world. First was a 3 dimensional tic tac toe set with glass marbles on 3 acrylic levels. I'd beat everyone, in total 3 in a row. Second was her broken plug-in alarm clocks, which I completely disassemble. When I would put them back together from memory only, I would have extra parts here and there, but the clocks again worked the 2 times it happened. I believe Grandma help nurture multi-dimensional thinking in me before I turned 8 years old. And she got me Simon for my 12th birthday.

My being thrilled as the intellectually odd man out became a distinct advantage in my life. An entrepreneurial career became my direction by 15 and carried the remainder of my life; thanks to this odd thinking.

At 47 I willingly immersing myself into street life, using a tent and sleeping bag for the first time in my life was by no means my most bizarre endeavor to date. Yet each life choice ending in success or failure has led to other abilities that could not exist without the previous events and their lessons. Life has shaped me into an individual that feels confident speaking on the subject of unhoused Americans, and providing some simple cures.

Winning my son Maxwell a copyright lawsuit against The Color Run would have never happened if not for my 1998 business loss of $185,000.00 in someone else's bankruptcy. I was green at the time, but following that loss I studied enough to never be helpless in a federal court again, gaining the ability to understand and act.

Had I not been falsely arrested and accused because of my being unhoused, the bias may not have become a hot button for me. Without Doug W White and Nicole DeJohn along with Jodi Lee Crawford and my moving to Denver, this manifesto would never have been my constant contemplation over the last 15 months of my daily walk.

– More Thinking Out Loud–

For almost a year here in Denver my words, spoken aloud have often been "I would love to fight that one in court" frankly this was not what I had in mind. But, it is very much what is at hand.

Two normal P.C. people, thinking they are righteously protecting their community by eliminating the riff-raff as self defined by their eyes and noses, disrupted my life and brain forever.

Ignorance to bias and discrimination is more easily understandable when you are separate from a discriminated group. Sympathetic to living on the streets is different when housed humans demonstrate charity. Former street dwellers contribute in a very different manner and with different motives.

From observation and constant inquiry over the past year I think that those who are impacted directly or by a loved one's disadvantage when offering charitable assistance is much more a pay it forward mentality. Where those removed from the "receiver group", just choosing their newest cause, this charity comes from a slightly less selfless place. Whether it be charity provided by organized Judeo-Christian groups for better ranking in heaven or by non-Church charity all are slightly misguided, because they are removed from the actual group they support. What I mean to imply is their goods and charitable services are on target, but the exploitation of measurable improvement in the lives of those they contact as a desired result. "Oh, look how many people we helped today." Their hopes are of fixing the grand problem. These ideals which I entertained in the past are now unreasonable to my mind. I now recognize the self serving deficiency in the equation.

Over the past 10-15 minutes I have pondered the previous paragraphs. Reason being, it is a brand new revelation to me with the current data plus experiences in my day to day and the past 40 plus years in the PC world. Those, along with never being part of a minority or lower class group as often referred, I lacked the ability to hypothesize with this level of accuracy! Given all current knowledge, my current situation being wrongly charged, and questioning motives that have no "greater good" in my belief. These "normies" should really not want to invest their time. But as I investigate my situation I discover darkness which I was ignorant to in the past and hadn't noticed this previous year; likely because this past year I was not outside for anything but the adventure and party. Yet the manifestation of the dog poop lady caused this level of over-thinking as well as hunting for the reasoning behind the various issue facing the homeless and other groups throughout history.

So it would be real to define those who give to any group they have not been elevated from the deficit of the group personally or observing loved ones within, their giving is self motivated and therefore scales to the side of selfish benevolence, "find a cause". Versus, those deprived as the minority themselves providing the charity, whether be illness by way of cancer or of standard race religion or economic deficiency/ poverty/ homeless. When those within a group or recently elevated, choose to provide charity to that same group their motive is solely conviction to contributing improvement within, not for personal standing or resume filler.

At a later date the above thought bares further investigation for support along with debate. Because it would likely, if accurate, provide that all oversight boards should only be comprised of documented members or past members of that specific group or minority. As well as dispelling the equality notion that middle class white and non urban social workers judge urban and black minorities in an uncontrolled negative way because they have no real knowledge of their situation first hand. Many of these simple truth concepts are evasive to smart people because they lack a much needed perspective to provide accurate support. There becomes no ability for human's to lack some level of selfish motives when selecting a charitable cause from a list. This includes myself, when choosing the charity to work with when I was 18, planning to organize an event with the 1969 New York Mets, I choose the Heart Association because Gil Hodges died of a heart attack. I chose for the event popularity only. The proceeds from admissions went to them, which was great and all but it was just money. I contributed for a business write off and boost recognition and credibility to my unknown event. However if my grandfather had died of a heart attack and I was unaware of Gil Hodges cause of death, then I would be directly attempting to impact the cure with my monetary contributions, and thus be a selfless selection, even though I would still be looking to coattail the Heart Association's name recognition giving credibility to my event, and that would be the self-serving byproduct and priority reason for giving any profits in the first place. Only the choice would be selfless not the associated benefit. But for me this was not the case it was 100% for the success of the Show. This is a very overtaking fact of prior blindness. Identification of this new information in my world, may have been overlooked if not for the existence of this case against me. Would I still be stuck on this in my head if it had impacted one of my "co-horts" and not me?

With my experiences in life I now have a willingness to accept that which I own no control. It is simpler for me to identify root issues and develop a clear picture, with a deep need to derive a new answer, with each new fact the outcome then changes. I now have the ability to wait and continue to gather information, not having an itch to gain instant results or correction of the injustice. In the past I would have been jumping to the D.A. and Governor by this point to employ swift correction of the provable wrongdoing.

It took me 49 years, to allow things to run their course, rather than looking to quickly rectify the wrong by yelling to point out the overlooked facts of the situation. I am hoping in the long run this newfound perspective no longer requires the need to bend steel to control outcomes, but allow the truth to prevail because control was surrendered.

Only life experience can enable my current patient behavior, this line of thought can only be learned in the living of life, period. Had I not been falsely accused, prosecuted and jailed years ago, there is no way I would be able to allow inaction to be controlling me. I would be yelling about the terrible police investigation of the situation, and perhaps looking to contact the accuser to correct it. Both of which are now seen by me as a waste of time and result in additional problems. I am willing now to wait for the police action and behavior of the accuser to be discredited in a trial forum.

Seems a large catch 22, understanding how to behave only after prior experience where such screw ups existed that it lands you in jail.

Jailbirds are also a group. All prison/jail boards responsible for lifestyle for inmates should consist of 50% minimum former inmates!! Digest that!!

As is postulated "it takes one to know one" equally I now believe I have strong accuracy in stating: "you cannot substantially improve a social or other minority from being treated as less without having belonged as a deprived member in that same category or minority group (excluding scientific breakthrough for medical groups). A white person defending rights of black minorities rings selfish to prove lack of bias. Yet if that white human is in a mixed relationship or parenting an adopted child of color which they witness being mistreated, they have ownership of the negative outcomes relating to the group and therefore have an authentic voice.

Previously I believed the logic of charity "feels good". A life including volunteerism and charitable events does in fact feel good, but there are many other fun and good feelings at non charitable events or working for pay. So where do these "feel good" notions originate? This good feeling is inside the giver's head, and imagination of betterment by their association to the benevolent group, and little more. This is truly self serving for the warm fuzzies of good deeds/hero affection.

We are one messed up civilization, I see clearer daily as I become willing to explore alternative ideas people call living. Being there is no schedule or pre-written script, we go into life with very little scope of the vastness of reality! It seems realistic to conclude that the few that genuinely empathize, feeling the wrongfulness of the prejudice affecting one group or another, cannot hold the same factual reality as one advocating from within the group or one degree removed from the negative effect.

Until you become the pre-judged and are victimized because of a grouping or categorization, you really are just guessing what to say or simply parroting someone else's words or feelings. I was less skeptical

89

of life and people prior to my Denver arrest. I offered much more credit to those who do provide by way of charity. Being well treated most of my life, yet only the past couple years falling into any judged group has been very eye opening, landing me on the receiving side of many verbal attacks. Only because I am a part of the grouping I am less because of a lack of roof, clearly false!

I should be outlining my case right now for my lawyer appointment next week but these thoughts continue to develop as the pen rolls over the page so I am going with it. Maybe this awareness could allow Max to be more effective in government? (Max, may oldest of 2 sons, called me at 19 and expressed interest in becoming President of The United States.)

Update – I am glad that even though the case was dismissed, I refrained from investing time in a lawsuit against White and DeJohn.

Because if I had filed a civil complaint and prevailed there surely would have been a non-disclosure clause and I would not be able to be writing most of what led me to my beliefs contained in these pages.

Entry Level Advancement
Addressing the Roots

Financial disarray is fast growing and the persistent problem our nation currently faces with un-housed Americans. The financial fiasco of the first decade of the 21st Century demonstrated to the world by way of U.S. banking and finance markets that middle and lower income stability is a myth. So many middle income earners were encouraged to spend above their means and had no wiggle room when things went bad. Only those with sound financial health first and foremost remain stable and often excel in tough volatile markets. We need to financially educate the impoverished Americans along with housing them within their current means.

Those who doubt that there are much better answers for keeping a roof over the heads of the financially ill equip, are those in the decision making power positions. These great intentioned decision makers have such a retarded view and little ability to effect long term positive outcomes to the masses.

Attempting to simply adjust the system of the 60's established for only those who have completely fallen short of achieving a stable life, which at that time were few and far between. And further it was rarely due to inability to afford housing while being employed 50 plus hours a week.

Select recent successes in housing street dwellers have been over hiped for political positioning, as well as being over funded, yielding the success illusion, for images of achievement and media purposes. These select handful are by no means the overall picture of reality to house Americas that are under employed, nor do they offer the long term solutions correcting the roots.

Even Utah, with great success housing the needy across the board, by using percentages that are statistically questioned when the full shelters and service resistant are counted. Critics point out the inaccuracies of percentages reported to media actually being more propaganda.

We must adjust our short sighted expectations and create long term implementation of imaginative and original corrections. This is not going to be a swift fix, but housing issues can be cured over the next two decades, provided tools and education to all those in danger of falling into financial disarray are delivered via multiple courses and reasonable housing built for low rent.

We all agree that the retail, food service and factory employees need to progress to a livable wage, yet they themselves lack the true education to do so.

We face two difficult problems, while retail and food-service employers cannot afford dramatic increases in minimum wage, they can afford increase stipulations based on time on the job. Provided the second problem is addressed, engagement in entry level education by the new-hire employee.

Rather than increase starting wage, or require overtime pay upon 40 hours, above true hourly value; impose legislature to require increase upon time in on the job. Offset employer costs by providing tax credits for retention of staff. As well as the employers recognized cost savings in training new staff versus retaining and duly promoting staff to a livable wage.

6 month increase with completion of entry level classes, 12 month increase can be within the $15 an hour range. For employees that have completed their entry level courses, being newly hired should only have to wait 90 before the 6 month pay standard is effective.

Classes will be administered in a similar manner as OSHA or continuing education classes for professional staff. Employees working 35 hours per week or less will be provided classes in exchange for

8 hours of volunteer hours per each of the 5 sections of the Entry Level Development Program. (Volunteer hours provided to Community Parks or Recreation Programs or otherwise determined at a later date). Those 35.01 hours or more per week will be provided the courses at no exchange of time, Department of Human Services funding can be redirected.

Courses to include:

101 - Checking/Banking (fee avoidance training)

102- Taxation (W4 exemptions, and other basics)

103- Credit Report and Establishment of Good Credit

104- Skill to Negotiate and Request Waiver of Fees, and Payment Plan/Arrangements. (beyond banks)

201- Resume Skills

202- Networking Importance - Burnt Bridge Reduction Skills

203- Providing Value to Your Employer

301- Finding Career Passion, not just work for working sake.

302- Profit and Loss Statements 101 small to medium business.

303- Personal Development - Think and Grow Rich Goal Setting Skills. (long and short term goal development)

401- Couponing and Savings Techniques

501- W. Edwards Deming's - 14 Point Workplace Outline

These 5 Entry Level Earner Programs will educate beginners thus providing life skills and added value to current and future employers. Pay may increase minorly upon completion of each segment, but not required.

Over a two decade progression, 100% of the workforce will have become much more skilled in the core understanding of how to not stay in entry level positions for long. Then communicating those life stories to the next generation, further encouraging a constant growth and upward development model.

Those working yet still below established livable wage thresholds including entry level 50 hour workers, SSI dependant disabled individuals, and other low income earners can be allocated supplemented rental assistance to live in the community they work.

If the data is close, costing upwards of $14,000 per year per unhoused person within a community, this redistribution of monies would be a savings overall and create a more stable future for all. We are all benefited if there are no members of our community sleeping in the streets for financial reasons. Our interconnection is a vital part of the United States and there is a large working population being left behind. If every property taxed within a community can divert the use of $100 per year to a fund, which can supplement up to $200 per month rent to individuals within the underpaid/fixed incomes that are below thresholds established as livable wage, within their community.

Classes for all entry level minimum wage earners, providing life skills which will prevent financial disarray, while providing current and future employers with additional value from the employee.

Denver/Occupy 2012
Urban Camping Ban Debacle

The Occupy protests in downtown Denver caused fear in residents, because the environment was antichrists and police haters, not just those feeling the financial inequity of the system.

From what I am told by many of my compadres' that were here and in other cities with Occupy, it became a festival environment throughout the US, where people harassed police, park goers, and the communities at large, they drank and did drugs all while camping in various communities around America. Where the travelers offered no true support to the movement, however added the bodies to the sizes of core groups nationwide and disturbed the delivery of their true message.

That the houseless numbers will increase and problems will follow if the inequities of the 1% upon the 99% continue. However this party and antichrist environment caused the messages to be very muddy.

The ban on urban camping in the City of Denver came about not due to the actual homeless population in the community, but because of Occupy. Because the residents and government no longer knew how to deal with the protesters that were camped out in the Civic Center Park. Closing the Park just pushed protesters to alternate areas closer to business and residents. The smallest % of elitist businessman and property owners along with City Council and support from the Mayor, passed the urban camping ban. It seems Americans have a long history of not liking people that live in tents.

The police training manual for Denver PD promotes the lack of enforcement of this arrest able crime, which the data below exemplifies. The SOP for police is to disrupt the behavior by means of harassment and aggravated contact with those sleeping outside is bizarre. Even when sleeping in a park during open hours, which is legal in Denver. This behavior on behalf of the City is gross and in my opinion poor conduct. The chart below shows 4 years of the actual contacts, demonstrating that officers do not enforce the law, they merely disrupt the law breaking behavior. Odd. I cannot imagine committing an arrest able crime witnessed by police and being told to *stop it,* and then encouraged to leave without penalty. The City is just causing more hopeless moments in these unhoused residents of their own community.

8,500 harassed, only 17 cited, not enforcing the laws.

Below is the proposal I presented to Denver City Council 12/15/2016 upon request from City Councilman Rafael

Espinoza, post the 4 year failure of The Urban Camping Ban of 2012, and recent national and international criticism of the tent, blanket and other property sweeps. I however am on the fence with the reasonableness of these clean ups. The below document is also a passionate rant to correct injustice I can see.

The Jackson Manifesto to City Council 12-15-2016- Alternative means of non-enforcement of DUCB

1. This document will be distributed by officers, Park Rangers and outreach workers, allowing those affected by houseless situations to feel comfortable within their Hometown of Denver.

2. This directive will allow those, perhaps at a low point of life, to rebound without intimidation or additional acrimony.

3. Proper application of this directive will demonstrate what can be accomplished when the city and their dislocated residents of Denver work together to improve lives, rather than causation of additional acrimony.

4. This directive is intended for reasonable individuals to act in a reasonable manner. We

recognize that many are against the urban camping ban for a number of reasons, yet just as many are in favor of the camping ban, including those compelled to enforce it.

5. If effective this directive will allow for follow-up with permanent adjustments within the existent statutes, rather than solely the DPD Training Manual.

6. If effective many, if not all the related statements of "It would be different if only they..." may be corrected.

7. - if they weren't trash collectors, sprawling rubbish everywhere, after it has been discarded for paid removal.

8. - if they weren't constantly leaving used needles around / openly using narcotics.

9. - if they weren't so often in the way of my attempts to: enter/exit businesses /freely walk the city.

10. - if their tents weren't in the way.

11. - if they would clean up after themselves without having to be asked (caretakers of their home)

12. - if they respected the city they live in.

13. Acceptance of the simple fact, we cannot easily answer the question "how can we eliminate houselessness." we will no longer attempt to discard our houseless residents, instead attempt to put our best foot forward and to befriend and assist our roofless neighbors, gaining insight needed to eventually end the cycle of houseless Denverites experiencing long or short term problems preventing them

108

from becoming housed and financially independent.

14. We recognize the American spirit of adventure and exploration, and accept that Denver is a hot-spot for many who travel the U.S.A. This directive will serve to inform the true transient **"which our houseless resident neighbors are not"** to become aware of the standards of roofless living in Denver.

15. We recognize that though many of the roofless have come to Denver because of marijuana law in some consideration factor, the percentages are not disproportionate to the overall population increase.

16. We have come to realize that the constant defaming of those without a roof, leaves a mark with each encounter, therefore we commit to "objective interaction" without judgment of the individual of their lack of a roof.

17. We recognize that the roofless of Denver are not all transient and having a shelter address on identification, prevents the use of such inaccurate terms in police reports or other official documents. It is not a label to be placed on a non-traveling individual or group.

18. Based on the complete failure of the current statutes enforcement, as well as costs to the community by way of inconsistent enforcement, questionable factors, destruction of life assisting gear of which much is gifted and donated to our local 501(c)3 outreach charities just days before, as well as the factual data that the Denver Urban Camping Ban has not in any way had a positive effect on housing all Denverites: We hereby propose "Denver City's Stay Safe Winter 2017". The DUCB will not be eliminated or yet re-written, nor is it to be repealed, we instead propose that if under the guidelines and standards presented here, which any reasonable person can understand, obey and self enforce; the fact that they are

roofless will be ignored. Therefore the roofless group or individuals will be let stay without "move on" request from law enforcement. Law breaking enforcement begins and or ceases at the scene with the primary officer. Officers are granted the ability to ignore non-domestic or non-violent petty offenses, this seems the ideal scenario to exhibit this positive and productive behavior of ignore the petty crime. With specific regard to human life and health we believe a 3 person or smaller tent or tarp shelter be able to stay for weather below freezing 32 degrees whether day or night.

19. We have learned much over the past 4 years and much will be reflected within this document.

20.   **CONDITIONS : SHORT LIST**

- Area free of rubbish. (non usable life supporting property)

- Structure and or individuals free of obstructing passing.

- Area free of narcotics both use or trafficking.

-Free of illicit underage marijuana consumption unless medical card in possession.

(over 21 users who have no permanent residence will be granted discreet consumption thus preventing potential Civil Rights Violations of the 8th Amendment as has been previously presented to the courts regarding public consumption and intoxication by alcohol of roofless individuals with drinking issues. We in Denver have laws in place for public display or consumption to mirror those of our Liquor Statutes and Regulation, and therefore will ignore discreet consumption of marijuana by those over the consumption age of 21. Warnings for non-discretion will be issued if overt consumption is observed in plain sight of officials.

-Free of public disruption or disorderly behavior by any group or individual.

21.   "Plain Sight -Probable Cause" standards will remain in full effect for criminal activity discovery.

22.   If no criminal behavior is reported to officers or observed by officials on scene, Denverites without

stable housing will not be considered a problem. But criminal activity will not be tolerated or ignored as a benefit of the houseless status. (With exception of consumption of marijuana as stated above.)

23. Complaints lodged against those without a roof will be looked at objectively by officials to be sure it is not an act of revenge or attempt to dislocate an already dislocated individual. If such complaint is an attempt to disrupt houseless behavior the courts will not facilitate such complaints. Threat complaints and harassment complaints against the houseless often end up in court without a complaining witness due to the simple fact the complainant no longer has the problem of this defendant in their sight, and have already achieved the task of further displacing that individual. City Prosecutors have become accustomed to saying "the victim(s) would rather just put this behind them" when their complaining witness fails or refuses to show for Trial. This entire behavior is 100% against the law to begin with, yet houseless individuals often get jailed, addressed as

transient (which they are not), and forced to make repeated appearances in court or face Warrant for their Arrest being issued by the Judge. This is not a victimless event, nor was the complaining witness credible to begin with beyond them having a residential address often in a million dollar plus high rise. While the defendant is registered at 2323 Curtis Street and becomes guilty on face value regardless of the factual basis. These situations will now be objectively investigated on the street, perhaps even calling in expert officers who are trained to positively interact with the un-housed preventing potential misunderstanding, and escalation from simple contact, to physicality or resisting arrests charges, which often carries on past the lack of the original complaining witness and dismissal of that related charge, but officers must support the charges they filed or face civil actions for lack of supporting evidence, even if the primary charges are deemed bogus and dismissed for lack of a witness.

24.   Those who are houseless often have tools in their possession which in other cases may be

considered weapons. Fixed blades exceeding 3 inches or bladed on both edges, Axes, Tomahawks, Machete, Hammers, just to name a few. If officials encounter roofless individuals possessing such tools, they will be given objective consideration to whether it is a tool used connected to survival or in fact just a weapon being wielded, this will be determined by its use, storage and the actions of the individual being questioned with regard to the object in question.

25. We recognize that many uncounted roofless Denver residents are in fact gainfully employed. By disrupting sleep with patrol car lights flashing cherries and berries as well as flashlight which often exceed 700 lumens which is blinding at best and beyond startling when tucked in a sleeping bag. There is not any possibility this action (which protects Officers) causes incentive to get back inside housing, nor the desire to get up and report to work and be productive with 3 or 4 hours sleep followed by degrading interactions at wee hours of the AM. Therefore enforcement of Camping violations will be

kept to the hours of 8am to 8pm for the period of this temporary directive.

26.   We recognize and understand the fact that street family is often formed for property watch and personal safety. Where only one person is left behind in an area where the belonging of many exist. Objective understanding should cause officials to move on themselves and return at a different time within their shift to address the original issue with the larger group, if trash or any other violations. More of the property owners can be addressed for whatever issue existed causing the original official concerns. But we see addressing one of five over property they are merely guarding does not get communicated the same objective way intended at first contact, causing additional acrimony to the absent group. There should be no issue with officials holding comment to swing back to the area if urgent enough.

27.   Facilitates for laundry services are few and far between and often wet weather drying of property will take place in public spaces. For purpose of this temporary directive this will be limited to Noon to

3pm unless cloud cover lifts after 12 pm, then 3 continuous hours will be granted to properly protect the individual overnight, with dry as possible coverings. *Additional consideration of funding, or providing laundry tokens may be a wise long term need of our roofless neighbors.*

28. All and any tents or other short term life protecting structures must be able to be collapsed upon request. Such request will only occur between 8am and 8pm unless criminal activity present. Requests to collapse structures will be only if, 1) above 32 degrees, and 2) the "free of" conditions above are unmet. If request made by law

enforcement it will be obeyed. Law enforcers will then provide a reasonable period for these individuals to correct the issues of unmet conditions of "Stay Safe" If unwilling to correct issues one hour will be granted to collect belongings and leave the area remaining in violation.

29.   If those residing in Denver can not comply with these simple standards they will be dealt with via littering citations and the Urban Camping Ban in place.

30.   We recognize the legal right for this who reside in Denver whether having a bed and roof or not, to the preservation of life and limb and desire to stay safe. Those without a roof also call Denver HOME!

31.   We move to pass this application of standards for Camping or violations of Denver City Parks Curfew along Cherry Creek and Platt Greenways, provided camping not in plain sight or attempts to obscure view of structures as well as meeting the conditions of standards above. Additionally, tents or temporary structures MAY NOT be erected on grass areas of Parks from 5am to 11pm, which will be dealt

with using current Parks 39:7(a) even if temperatures are below freezing. We have determined through direct observation of Parks Department Rangers as well as Denver Police, there is a smaller percentage of dislocated individuals who have taken temporary residence within the Parks and mainly the Greenways along the Platt and Cherry Creek Trail, this behavior remains frowned upon, yet if tents remain obscured or camouflaged from plain sight, this non-egregious violation will be ignored, provided the above "Standards of Denver City Camping" are followed. If the Standards are followed, the observing Ranger will thank individuals or groups for being "stewards of the land" keeping it maintained for all to enjoy free of rubbish. Also making trash bags available.

32. Parks and City workers will provide the exact services to those un-housed as other Denver residents that use the Parks by providing removal of trash secured in bags placed clearly but not obstructing the right of way, along the curb or next to other trash cans or receptacles along Cherry Creek and the Platt River.

Properly bagged trash will no longer be ignored as if it were offensive to Parks Staff to assist in maintenance of the grounds.

33.   Parks will not be used after Curfew for anything but "Safe Stay" this includes but not limited to no loud music, no fire pits or grilling, no roaming, expectation of sleep from 11pm through 5am will be the additional condition within Park Property, as well if these violations do occur the individuals failing to obey lawful orders from Rangers will be dealt with, utilizing the current 39: codes established for these infractions at their discretion, Administrative Citations will be issued, and police will be contacted with information regarding such infractions.

34.   We recognize and unquestionably agree that perception is often much more germane than reality or best intentions. With this reasoning, we have been made aware that a speculative proposal has been tossed around to provide a Safe Stay Space within Denver at various available City controlled properties, including perhaps the vacant unutilized Coors Field Parking Lots downtown. We are aware

that those who dwell indoors may have the best intentions with these proposed options of assistance, yet such large scale approved places will no doubt be perceived as Concentration Camps of the 40's or even evoke belief that it is being orchestrated by Federal Management Systems thus will fail to address the issue without again, creating larger more negative backlash to the reputation of Denver as a whole. All and any plans to corral or confine an entire class of individuates in specified spaces, especially fenced and or surveilled will further deteriorate trust and halt advancement of those being forced to use such assigned spaces. Such plans will no longer be considered a viable alternative or potential safer fix for individuals displaced, regardless of the good intentions of the housed advocates making such suggestions.

35. We are asking for those displaced residents of Denver be "Let Stay" without additional acrimony due to criminalization of their lacking a permanent address within the City. Provided these individuals

are good neighbors and caretakers of the areas occupied. Any less will be met with swift correction or enforcement of current Statutes on within the law.

36. For humanitarian reason and the retention of some level of autonomy, we hereby give Right to transient individuals, and roofless Residents of Denver who have been displaced from housing either long or short term to only be judged as criminals if actual criminal behavior is observed or reported, not for their residential challenges or dilemmas, to include sleeping in cars or in public spaces while being respectful and following the above conditions demonstrating desire to be good neighbors within Denver.

37. No property take notices will be distributed during these 90 days, unless correction of the above conditions are ignored after tickets for littering have first been issued, with 24 hours given to correct the issue (preventing a double jeopardy prosecution from being imposed). Follow-up will be noted in daily logs to provide additional support for or against this temporary directive and whether ticketing for litter

affects any overall positive improvement within the community of unhoused, knowing that ticketing for camping has not delivered any measure of improvement over the past four years since 2012.

38.   Littering tickets will be issued to anyone staying within an area deemed containing excess litter, if those individuals correct the issue to a reasonable standard, tickets **may be voided** by the issuing officer or direct supervisor upon request, further removing the burden of the courts and jails for enforcement of the same.

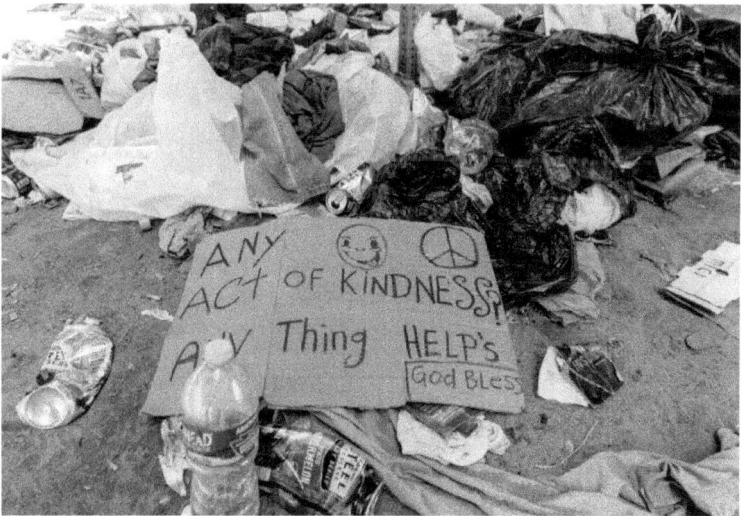

39.   Affecting the larger problem of those dislocated from housing will take work and creativity on all

parts. Those dislocated, the City and State Government, and most of all other Denverites who do not have to weather the sub zero Denver nights: all must be heard. We must realize the un-housed stay because they have their own reasons as well because those living outside in winter, spring, summer, or fall believe in their soul that their home just as your, is Denver Colorado period. By understanding this simple truth we bridge the gap and open pathways for communication and solutions rather than the continuous downgrading of human spirit and hope, making way for real long term solutions for correction of this unpalatable circumstance being faced by so many, for such a vast array of causation that each case must be addressed as unique and serviced with action plans that are specific to the needs of the recipient not the simple application of stock solutions across the board. We must begin a grassroots effort to eliminate the root causes of dislocation via per-eviction assistance and cutting of red tape for those who can be rescued with considerably less of an investment of City resources or finance. Often a few hundred dollar unexpected expense or similar event will cause families to be evicted or individuals to fall short even though they are maintaining long term employment, paying taxes and being a positive force within their Denver circle. This can be quickly and inexpensively addressed, yet the time required for stopgap funding tends to exceed the window of the courts. Thus landlords rights are supported and lawful eviction soon follows without ability for remedy within the small window where emergent needs arise and funding is available but too late. Americans and Denver residents living paycheck to paycheck due to increasing expense and stationary pay scales are often one unexpected bill away from being out of their permanent domicile. A single assistance extension of $500 to $1,000 could with minor financial planning, provide a stopgap measure providing families or individuals with a future 12 months of stability and prevent interruption of employment, social status, education of adults or children as well as lessening long term burden of assistance programs and landlord tenant court Dockets.

40. We recognize that we have no way of knowing the mindset nor motivations of those who remain unhoused in this deathly cold weather. But we do know we can no longer prevent life enhancing assistance. Our community 501(C)3 charitable business have collected and distributed tens of thousands of dollars in camping gear and life protecting blankets tarps cloths and other much needed protection from the elements of Denver to only have that donated property discarded by either Parks staff or City contractors tasked to remove the property of those using public spaces. This cycle will stop today and property will not be confiscated or discarded if it is in public spaces either being overseen by an assigned proxy, or if it is unattended in areas free of :litter, rubbish and excess non life supportive property, neatly. Shopping carts and other stolen property will be confiscated on sight for fingerprinting and potential theft charges being filed if investigations support such charges. This will also

apply to any plain sight item which the holder clearly has no right extended to posses such item off the property of origin. Such stolen property will be made know to the rightful owners for best chances of return if such owner information is available.

41.   We the undersigned hereby agree to this 90 day directive be endorsed for humane reasons of preservation of life and limb of our displaced neighbors within Denver.

42.   We understand we have counted in excess of 600 service resistant individuals living on the streets, yet they're registered utilizing little if any services issued to these residents of Denver.

43.   To better attempt to understand, we support the "Stay Safe" proposal because it will work to better all trained outreach workers offering services without the constant need search out clients because they have been told to relocate; if they want less aggressive and less frequent contact by police or other enforcers they will become better neighbors. Yet these law enforcers actually are instructed to "only" roust those sleeping

in public spaces via intimidation and threat, so there are no Constitutional challenges if officers perhaps pick on someone like "Jackson" this preventing challenge of the Ban and or Class Actions for criminalization of status as houseless with no permanent address in a private domicile.

44. This proposal will allow improved and more successful completion of service applications, and identification processing, As well the new "judge objectively" not as if there is surely crime being committed solely based on sleeping outside or violations of park curfews. This basic order to law enforcers will compel all to deal with each case positively and treat displaced residents with ultimate respect, lifting spirits, as one would extent positive words to a second date if you plan on having a third.

45. We recognize a simple tent made of nylon or a standard tarp as a canopy A-frame across a string does in fact provide life enhancing protection for humans in the elements of winter at this latitude and elevation. Therefore, agree that if the conditions above are met Denver residents will not be disrupted

by officials on the basis of temporary shelter or sleeping mummified in a sleeping bag even if violating Park curfew. Services will continue to be made available to those who abide by this directive and outreach will maintain better communication with our citizens in need of their expertise. We also recognize that tents protect property and abate rodents and diseased insects, thus improving daily quality of life through preventive measures taken by the tent owners and they will be let be, if good neighbors and follow the conditions above.

45. Discontinuing sweeps and Parks removing personal property, whether attended or just hidden/camouflaged will improve the community with those living outside. When the Police or Parks discards sleeping materials, many get angry and lash out by stealing the same property from the next guy. This behavior is criminal, yet only exists because of actions first taken against them, causing them to believe if the City can steal their property, it's fine to steal from

other houseless folks as evidenced by the Cities prior actions.

46.   Dialog should be pleasant and brief. To include at least a referral # for services if requested. Trash bags available when possible (stored in cruisers and saddlebags of bike officers). Dialog to include complimentary words of encouragement if the conditions are met without argument or ticketing for litter. This can nurture the relations between City workers and those living in public spaces where these city workers perform their employment duties.

47.   We recognize that humans are resistant while experiencing houselessness for many varied reasons including but not limited to fear, pride, embarrassment, just to name a few. Fear of the camping ban itself can further drive someone into a deeper hole, emotionally as well as financially. Therefore this fear must first be addressed to best serve ourselves and those un-housed.

48.   Being on constant edge while sleeping, one ear open for police and rangers does not provide enhancement of any situation, therefore if the above

conditions are met, contact will be left to the hours of 8am to 8pm by officials.

49.   In temperature above 32 degrees tents and or any temporary shelter should be disassembled and carried with or stored neatly out of pathways not causing obstruction or eyesore of any kind. If such obstruction does exist the owner risks loss of property under law.

50.   Complaints to officials from within an occupied area against one or more of the group will be primarily dealt with as domestic by virtue of sleeping proximity, whether the initial complaint comes from within or outside by a bystander. This will leave police with little room to not arrest and or issue restraining orders against those involved, preventing cohabitation and or return to the area of the incident. This would scare most straight, preventing many petty internal alterations because even housed people fear any possibility of getting tangled up into domestic law, it is just not the place anyone but divorce attorneys want to be!

This document in its entirety has been authored by Eric T Jackson, a 27 month Denver resident, currently living outdoors as an individual directly aware of the overall issue from both sides. Jackson for the past 2 years has lived the first 14 months without residence for the first time in his 48 years. Then resided in Park Hill until November 15, 2016 due to domestic disputes with the roommate where he was co-leasing a two bedroom 600sq ft apartment in a 4 plex. Recently turning 50, he has made it his mission to somehow enhance the daily lives of all sides of what he considers to be some of the worst interactions between those in need and those in power, he has ever directly witnessed.

Jackson was the previous owner operator of a number of privately held pizza delivery restaurants in Southern New Jersey. He has the belief, as a "Normie" for his first 45+ years, along with his 30+ years of business successes and failures, combined with his complete immersion into the roofless and Stoner Hill communities 12 continuous months upon arriving in Denver, he is providing a very workable and comprehensive stopgap proposal attached. In consideration of this document he has examined the reality of his past two years, questioning officials on a constant basis to evaluate the situation and hopes to improve the number of positive interactions between his street family and the other hundreds of Denver Residents who endure homelessness in Denver and the City in a whole.

Jackson is well known to Sgt. Vincent Lombardi, and all the off duty officers working the Commons Park security detail. Jackson considers these officers as peers, offering him a wealth of factual information with regard to marijuana law and issues, as well as the overall behaviors of officials towards displaced residents. His passion and desire for positive outcomes by reducing the imposition of fear as the tool currently being used most often with regard to camping in Urban Denver. He agrees a level of fear keeps people safe; but in this situation it provides no safety" it only causes additional acrimony for all involved. Jackson is also well visible around the Stoner Hill area, and known to most Parks dept. Staff including the Rangers.

Jackson says he had all intentions of starting a business in Denver or the surrounding area when he arrived, after leaving his north east roots. He found himself awed by the lifestyle of those who traveled the country and those who were monopolizing the Hill in Commons Park at Little Raven and 16th street. He says had he continued his last business, selling and installing security cameras for small to medium businesses, he would have learned very little in his last two years beyond variations in permitting in Colorado vs. NY, NJ and Philadelphia. But, because already retired in his mind and working to author and publish two additional non-fiction books under his publishing company A.D Echo Publishing Foundation established for his first book in 2012, hanging out homeless in Denver would offer an exciting adventure that his life lacked as a goal driven successful entrepreneur for the prior 30 years. He believes now there was greater purpose and universal influences that cause him to follow this path as long as he has, even though other options may have presented themselves. He believes this proposal being offered herein was the true reason he was lead to this path of living homeless in Denver. His full emersion allows him to combine all his prior experience and creativity to the above offered improvements for the Denver Camping Ban Debacle.

Jackson has two sons from a short 7 year marriage, 23 and 24 year old boys, one graduating FAU in Boca Raton today 12/15/2016 as he offers this proposal and the other scheduled to graduate FAU in December of 2017. Both Jackson's sons are aware of his homeless status and support the efforts their father is making to better the situation surrounding Denver's roofless.

Jackson acted on behalf of his older son pro-se in a federal court case, Maxwell W Jackson the photographer that The Color Run made the mistake of infringing on his art, eventually settling the case for $165,000 and photo credits after a yearlong battle in court.
Using his half century of specific knowledge learned by hard knocks and a few great mentors in the last two years, he has attempted to comprehensively and accurately cover all angles of the related issues of

DUCB lack of enforcement upon those he feels are most in need of a hand up not a kick out.

He believes deeply that correction of these issues begins by changing the tone from "ewe make them leave", to how can we help better everyone's quality of life impacted by the current failure of the DUCB.

Most recently Jackson reached out to the ACLU providing connection to and now representation of adults being issued Park area restrictions due to public display of marijuana. He became enraged that a Denver Police Officer or Park Ranger can switch hats and become judge and jury, imposing instant 90 day sentences, restricting freedom of movement, to alleged offenders in advance of due process for marijuana misuse. The Trespass case of Jackson friend Troy Holm, will go to trial on February 22, 2017 and is being defended by Adam Frank Esq. representing the ACLU.

Jackson had been labeled many things in his community on Stoner Hill Denver from all the different sides, Police, Rangers, waterfront residents and his stoner buddies on the Hill, but he just considers himself a caretaker with a brain and inspirer of goals and good character.

Background interview of Jackson by: Sandra Jeane Watson

Manifesto by: Jackson

Housing Needs

-My 2017 Goals: Raise **100 million** dollars in seed finance to create a 30 story building here in downtown Denver with units mostly 100 sq feet and no larger than 150 sq feet renting for 25% below SSI checks of seven hundred or so monthly. A bond offering in the City could facilitate this project. Teaming up with the VOA, Salvation Army or Coalition for the Homeless here in Denver would be great too.

-Zero parking, because parking facilities exist throughout the city. If you can afford a car, rent for parking is part of that responsibility and not available in this entry level housing.

-Bike racks within the common rooms on every floor.

-Small enough land parcels that all apartments are perimeter located with central common rooms on each floor. With stationary basic décor.

-Ride share bikes and cars on the 2nd floor, retail on the first. Third floor designated to co-location of service providers of transitioning residents, until such time that the third floor can be converted to apartment units.

-Give the investors 100% of the equity in the finished project taking 0 for myself, provided the development is named The Jackson Initiative.

My bedroom growing up on Long Island was 12 by 15 with two twin beds, desk, dresser, play area, 4x4 corner table, a closet, double window and alcove for my toy box. Single and 50 I could live in that space with losing half for kitchen and bath. Japan tiny apartments approx 75 sq feet are smaller than my bedroom.

Cheaper housing in America is in great need but is not likely without incentive, because supply and market demand pricing is in full effect. Also the keep up with the Jones/Rothschild's, meaning if I design and or build it, then it has to be bigger and better, whether the architects of a 30 story building or the private person having a house build from the ground.

Thus, popular areas will continue to push those earning minimum incomes, out.

There is a reason for diversity in the our community as well as our nation, it enriches all involved. We are a diverse and interdependent culture, and it needs to remain this way, even with financial imbalance.

Unless developers are extremely forward thinkers or provided incentives to build smaller units in taller buildings this problem of the unhoused in America will persist.

This corrective measures comes from someone who grew up in a 1500 sq ft 4 bedroom house, a tent of late, and a jail cell for 89 day while I wrote my first book. Also my being aware of Japan's micro apartments drives this thought. As I see it there is a serious lacking of entry level housing in the majority of prosperous areas of America.

The simple fact is there are no longer places for 18 year olds to move out to. Even when minimum wage was $3.15 when I started with Dominos Pizza in 1985, I was still able to rent a house with some friends and all of us were able to handle the bills. Once I was trained and at management levels within 6 months I would have been able to live solo in the area.

The loss of the entry level rentals has caused a radical number of young Americans to choose to be "Home Free" and live on the streets with little care. Many get into trouble with shoplifting or drugs, depending who they end up surrounding themselves with. These situations further tangle them up in the world of social, financial and judicial disorder. These free living individuals are not impressed with the standard of: get a job, work until you're dead in order to pay the bills, have nothing left over, no time to breath beyond working for someone earning wages.

Now on the other hand if Home Free youth were offered a closet sized apartment with the autonomy of a private entrance they would get a job and pay a rent as high as $475 a month while earning a minimum wage, just because of the autonomy. Many of the people that are on the streets are not able to live successfully with others. And often, their parents no longer willing to tolerating them at home living free, based on the standards of after 18 I am no longer responsible to my child. Pushing them out the door regardless of whether their child is ready or equip to be moving out. This leads to sleeping on friends couches and floors which tends to be a very short lived process before they are on the streets, having no idea what to do in order to correct the situation they find themselves.

My vision is to have "where available", high rise 20 to 30 story towers with entry level single living dwellings that are no more than 100 to 150 square feet. If you have not yet seen this style of living you should search You Tube "small apartments Japan" and take a quick look at the manner of living that other earthlings function within. Not having to be big in order to accommodate living. A single person truly can occupy and utilize minimal space happily, as long as they are able to rationalize the small space having an equivalently small price tag. I visualize for my area of Downtown Denver a 30 story building with upwards of 1500 units for singles without cars to occupy, from $500 to $575. An equivalent 30 story building being erected with a $100 million dollar project budget, resulting in a total of 288 livable units is very nice, but silly in a time when thousands of units are very much available but not occupied but for high pricing.

My $100 million dollar project would provide 1500 livable units, as entry level living. Denver has been approached by houseless charities to allow tiny home villages, which in my mind is a bizarre waste to have a property with a bunch of tiny club house sized structures. When the root reasoning is an attempt to correct the housing issues. Begin building up and occupying the property with one building that has many hundreds of units vs. a tiny village of dozens of units among other 30 story buildings and skyscrapers. It is a token effort at most on the part of community organizers and the local governments that they are working on projects for tiny home villages. To entertain the idea is foolish.

What would be the affect of a 30 story 1500 unit building?

1) There would be an immediate increase in 2 and 3 bedroom dwelling availability, where roommates share housing but really wish they could afford space of their own, freeing up rentals for family's

2) There would be an abundant number of street dwellers collecting only SSI and food stamps, providing the ability to be indoors within weeks of availability.

3) Social services assisted individuals would be able to affordable housing, thus setting these clients up with real chances to progress and establish themselves in stable long term housing situations. Many could exit the welfare assisted situation fairly quickly. Lowering the number of people ending up on the streets after the programs for short term housing assistance run out.

4) The excuse for street living would no longer be the complete lack of affordable dwellings, or need for high paying jobs.

5) Kids getting thrown out at 18 or leaving their family home for various reasons at a younger age with incomes lower than needed to live in the community they deem home. Where they have other support beyond the family unit, would now have a place to live at a very affordable cost.

6) This would allow entry level workers to dwell within the community where they are employed.

7) Nothing would prevent these individuals living in the tiny apartment buildings from wanting to progress in life and eventually graduate into larger housing. Thus freeing up the affordable housing to future generations. Constantly cycling lower wage earners into the autonomous stable adult living environment.

8) Inspire other condo and apartment builders to consider 5 times the number of units, at 1/4 the price; yet nearly the exact same overall construction costs because of lower end amenities and proof of function.

9) Provide better overall balance within communities by providing for this type of development within their master plans.

10) Provide livable space for divorcing couples or battered individuals remaining in poor situations just because of the inability to find housing at any reasonable cost.

My line of thinking is so very un-American because we tend to only think on the stage of constant improvement advancement and bigger is better. Tiny dwellings are required if we are to truly address the houseless crisis in America. It will become irrelevant to require developers to offer low income housing among their development or be fined. Regardless many just take the monetary fine and avoid providing the housing. That is the American way. Yet if we would just start out with a blank slate to think of ways to make it affordable for fixed income, low income, or entry level earners, along with youth estranged from their family homes to rent small apartments, it's a win win. It would become very reasonable to build an abundance of high rise buildings with thousands of basic 100 sq foot dwellings fully functional apartments to provide stable permanent address and shelter for all those who would choose to be inside today if the option existed within a price range affordable to $750 SSI check monthly and low income earners.

I see every window on the newly constructed skyscrapers in downtown Denver as single dwelling, allowing for large central common rooms on every floor. Apartments would run the perimeter of the building, measuring 7 ft wide, and 15 ft to 20 ft deep, with 14 ft ceilings allowing for loft bed and large overhead storage. Set up to be energy saving and green in every way possible. Entry level living communities would be car-free, so no parking is provided in the design. Excessive bi ke racks, perhaps multiple levels of the ground levels just to provide adequate bicycle parking that would be on video 24-7 for security, and car share spaces incorporated within the bike storage areas.

Possibly encourage non-profit high-rise housing in every major city in America. If VOA or other charities were encouraged to develop a 20 story 1000 unit apartment building with a small footprint, their ability to not need profit on the property construction, the expense would be lower than the average sq ft cost in the same community.

- Builders possibly given tax credits to triple or more, the number of units within a project. Constructing high-rise Japanese style tiny apartments, 8 square meters. 14' ceiling loft bedding above 8' standard mark, allowing non claustrophobic dwellings with overhead sleeping area and potential for overhead storage shelving. Provide large common rooms, on multiple floors, for various community activities.

Beyond House building:

Next rapid fix is a rather socialist concept I'm told by my son Maxwell, though I have no further addenda.

$100 of each property taxed allocated to a supplemental fund for low income workers living within a community providing service to others at least 50 hours per week yet still below the income needed to rent or live within the community they serve. Offer up to $200 per month to those low income individuals, and not push for increases in the minimum wage which could damage small business as a whole. Short term this may burden towns use of property tax, but long term will save on welfare, courts, and shelter housing as well as Detox and E.R. visits.

The most dangerous phrase in the language is "we've always done it this way."

Set Up For Failure Later

-to those who advocate minimum wage increase.

There are many who will advocate to increase the minimum wage. Yet, as a 20 plus year employer of entry level employees I whole heartedly disagree. There is no place for anyone to tell me what I should be paid, or pay someone to begin with, at a job that they desire. If I were to charge someone $500 to work for me the first two weeks, that should be my business as a businessman and a prospective employee. Further to be expected to increase a pay scale for anyone working over 40 hour is even more crazy. They were only worth X dollars for the first 40 and at the 41st hour how can they possibly be worth one and a half times that value.

My vision for a stable living wage is to only require a business to provide a minimum after 180 days on the job, and after completion of the entry level classes as described within. 90 days if classes already completed in prior job.

-Kids no longer get working papers and jobs at 15

This is the real problem with minimum wage standards and mis-information in the job market. There is a standard in the current market that allows employees under the age of 20 to start a job at 4.25 per hour for the first 90 days.

This is such an under promoted bit of information in the employer market that many I have asked had no idea. I was not aware of this standard at the time I was employing people, only after that point was I informed by an accountant that this youth sub-minimum wage even existed. For this reason and other expectations from the new hire as well as the competitors, prevents businesses from truly understanding and making use of this sub-minimum wage loophole. For me as an employer I was not aware of this factor and it in fact caused me to hire youth "off the books" and pay them cash for their first few months. If the minimum starting wage was completely eliminated and employers like me were given the ability to hire a green, untrained individual at whatever wage they mutually agreed upon would then allow me to pay a person I choose to keep after the first 180 days a wage that would be able to provide a better standard of living. I would almost think I could afford to pay someone $15 an hour as long as I was able to work them 50 hours a week without having to increase this wage at 40 hrs.

Eliminating minimum wage would cause our youth of America to get back to learning work related responsibility at the younger ages. Correcting their thoughts of being unemployable and the employer from choosing to not employ kids, for one reason or another. It would also prepare the youth for work and life outside of the continuing education system if that is their choice. Making every American choosing to work for someone else better worthy of the job, with a more functional wage structure for the employer and the employee.

When a new hire, who could possibly burn down my business in his or her first weeks of training is expecting constantly increasing minimum wage standards to be met in their new hire capacity it makes it difficult to not want a more seasoned individual to employ. Thus preventing many positions that would be better suited for the entry level trainee, are not offered or even considered at the pay rate expected.

Eliminate minimums and rebranding pay minimums to become something that is only implemented upon completing continued education as described. Employees will be providing a value to the employer with a level of understanding and desire for improvement.

This could help to turn around the inability of acquiring an affordable dwelling for a basic retail or food service position, once on the job six months.

-Pay comes in experience and training first, and money follows (today the value of internship has been lost). A respect level connected to getting a job at a young age has been dissuaded from the thinking of developing Americans. Concentrate on your studies, don't go to work at 15, they need to learn how to do both. There are no jobs delivering news papers anymore for kids, it's a grown-ups 3rd job applied for to afford the 15 year olds hobbies. There are no kids begging to work because they simply want to. I would bet the data on working papers issued to teens in America has dropped by greater than 50% over the past 20 years.

The lesson of being sent home from work a 15 years old, are simply lost. The impact of our first screw ups at our first job come way too late to have life impacting wisdom moments. Good habits provided by employers via standards and discipline are lost to the youth of our Country at this time. First employers are often like great teachers in school, remembered for a lifetime and provided tidbits of wisdom very much needed for a productive life. These are root problems, currently developing a society of youth choosing the streets and wandering through life with a feckless existence. Radical change is needed to improve this segment of the unhoused population as a large growing percentage that will continue if unchecked.

Additional rapid fix, anyone employed who ignored the instructions within the w-4 completed at hire, often fall into debt if they claim single 0 while making below taxation requirements to begin with. These individuals should be able to file a single online form allowing not just the change of status to their withholding but in their next check receive back all the in trust tax money paid to date, perhaps keeping them from becoming displaced from their housing situation on the spot.

Hakuna Matata

Dis-proportionate conviction rate

What did the houseless man wear to court? Nothing, because he didn't go, he couldn't get anyone to watch his property and he had nowhere to safely store it. Surely you cannot bring 4 duffel bags into the court house, you might have a nail clipper or pocket knife. What did he wear to his failure to appear hearing, whatever color the jail put him in because it took him getting arrested to make it to the court. And he lost all of his belongings, inevitably anyway. What did he plead once he got to the judge. Guilty, because the DA offered time served for sleeping under the bridge and the failure to appear with minimal fines, because he could not pay the bill anyway.

The houseless are often stopped and questioned having their names run for warrants and searched with little if not false cause. One of my favorites has become you match the description of a suspicious person I received a call about.

In addition to the prior story of my false arrest by Denver Police to spark this developing manifesto, I have also been detained three different times here, without cause. The most recent the officer told me to make sure I didn't stay in the parks after hours and get another curfew ticket, as his salutation when I finally chose to leave them alone and stop arguing the stupid reasons they were giving as cause for my arrest. They hate when someone knows what they are doing and are not able to be arrested.

Dis-connected from news and current events!

For me, it was in 2005 that I just stopped watching the news broadcasts. I am guessing that it was right after the Katrina hurricane and the news stations advertising the uses for bath salts, while not pointing out that the current banking and housing boom were fake and would never be able to last.

Yelling at the TV was enough for me to quit. I am not the person to quit anything, but the news was just to absent of needed truth for me to continue watching. I had little need to be apprised of current events while owning a pizza place. If something major was happening there was always customers that would communicate the breaking news and its potential impact. I was just so tired of hearing such useless information, and harmful facts that it became overwhelming, and that was just not the place for me to gain any knowledge of value. Things like informing the general public, who were clueless, that a product called bath salts could be bought over the counter in many places and offer the effects of crack cocaine when smoked, and were very dangerous, warning people not to buy this product, and not consume it. Now most people seeing the product would decide if they wanted to take a bath using such a product. If the news never broadcasted the drug factor hundreds if not thousands of sales would have been nonexistent. The news for me became more harm than good, more pointless information about death, rape, celebrity abuse of spouse and the like.

There was little information providing inspiring current happenings.

I know that at 40, I was not the only of my circle that just quit believing or relying on news for anything but false information and the evil of the world being reiterated again and again. There were no good reasons to any longer tune into the broadcast news or depend on news papers, because they were really not reporting anything that humans should expose their brains to anyway.

I have found that this is case regarding the subject of houselessness in the current state, the causes, and real discussion of curative measures are not covered in the news. When the unhoused are brought up, I catch it later on the internet after being told to watch, but the information is still mostly out of context and or 100% the opposite of what I witness on the streets. Here in Denver, as a person on the streets, and in the news for the advocacy of measures for improvement, I can tell you that the news could help the situation of the houseless. But when it is discussed there are bold misrepresentations. The biggest being use of the word "encampment". It is a redundant example of failure in my mind, on the part of broadcasters need to overstate rather than report. An encampment is in fact a military or like structured and fortified area to exchange war. Why would camping become not camping because it is on a city street? Why does the term : tent city function in areas where living outside in public in not yet criminalized, but in places where laws against houseless living the word describing a dozen tents (a camp or squat as it is know on the streets) becomes elevated to an encampment? BECAUSE IT SOUNDS ALARMING!

Dis-respected in their minds

Many elders will agree that the youth of the new millennium lack a level of manners and wonder why! But they stop there, just wondering, without inquiring or investigating or much more then complaining about the youth.

There is no doubt that a growing number of young adults lack many developed skills, including but not limited to manners and general respect for their elders. This is more likely because their parents have never been in a stable enough position to have the time or positive outlook to provide the support, direction or outside activities that yield mentorship of good, moral and positive behaviors. The last 20 plus years, youth feel they should be reporting their parents to police because they get smacked once for a dreadful outburst they think is justified.

However a truly abused child, would never even consider speaking out loud regarding the abuse they endure, let alone express that they should call the cops on the guardian that beats them.

Where does this attitude come from in these kids? Again the excessive broadcasting of never let anyone hit you, from school to TV. Parents have lost a level of ability to instill the fear of "dad's gonna kill me" "mom's gonna kill me" beliefs. This shift has caused kids to wrongly interpret discipline and direction as lack of parental respect. They often feel like their needs and desires are being ignored by parents. And the parent is at a loss to invent new means of reward and punishment to demonstrate what is good and what is bad, what is nice and what is mean and why. Parents deliver less information on how the child's behavior impacts others and the way they are perceived, because the parent themselves are ignored by the inattentive child and have little power to change the outcome. Rolling in the era of drugging school aged children. I interact today with many under 25 that are addicted to street drugs and pharmaceuticals' and I calculate over 75% of these addicts were on adderall and/or ritalin in their school age years. Shortly after came the antidepressants for kids exhibiting any signs of sadness. Those that were not drugged that I encounter as addicts living on the streets had other tragedy in their lives that led them to be estranged from family support and led to drugs or drinking by those they chose to become involved with on the streets.

There is no such thing as a gateway drug, it is an invented propagandized concept. The singular thing that is the gateway to most bad behavior are acquaintances "gateway people". The people that you expose yourself to, are always the ones that expose you to new ideas or behaviors, even if only a sit com cast of a favorite show. Gateway people can offer failure as easily as mentor success.

Drug gateway people are those that expose someone to a substance they have never used and demonstrate that consumption is not deadly and most times described as amazing.

I have smoked pot since 18 and not before, and drink rarely, at no point have I been dependant on any drug besides tobacco which I didn't start until divorce at 30 and hate that it got a hold of me. Not to imply I have not dabbled with many of the drugs out there, but again only when the person I most engage with is already in possession of the drug or drink.

For me no drug or drink was as inspirational as marijuana, providing me altered thinking that was beneficial in creative successes. Every other drink and drug was pretty much ingested to fit in and in considerable moderation, the rare times I do participate.

The youth of the streets, in their minds, have been lied to, and all promise of support, love and success has been taken away for some reason or another. There is not a single one of the youth on the streets that would not go get an entry level job if housing was only $475 a month here in Denver, while not having to deal with roommate bull shit. But with the high prices of housing and the low pay of entry level work causes them to become home free. They stay in their community of friends and various family yet, they live free on the streets because they feel in control. Not working for someone else, slaving in their mind for non-livable pay check. Being on the streets becomes their adventure for the moment, but they would gladly trade it in, for a stable existence. They see no direction which delivers them stable work, pay or housing so they give up and enter street life.

Their belief of no respect is not far from true. I only say this because the 20/20 hindsight demonstrates their parents did not have the stability of their grandparents or great grandparents in America. This inequity from generation to generation has left many of the youth on the streets to have little hope of owning a house, car, or existing without assistance from social services. Because this is the case, they say "FUCK IT", I'll stay on the streets. If no one comes into their lives to motivate and educate them to the reality of "behavior yields outcome", they may never get off the streets and stable.

Each and every young person on the streets that was born here in America not educated or raised correctly for one reason or another, whether in the system or not, were let down by those entrusted to provide them a productive future.

Isn't that the ultimate disrespect of a human being. So is there any wonder why they choose the life of leave the past behind you, live where ever you lay your head, no job, no boss, no bills, no responsibilities, and simply no worries .

Long term we're glad that Simba expressed clearly enough that it is good to take responsibility and to be the best you can, living up to the expectations of the society in which they live with veracity and good character. Although no worries, may be a great thing while in a stable home as a child, in a stable home teen agers are held to standards and expected to be able to live up to them, or lose privileges.

There is not a single person under the age of 30 that I have encountered in my 2.5 years interacting with 90% unhoused youth that came from a loving stable home. Lots of foster care, or family service involved in their lives, many abandoned to grandparents or other relatives, many with addict parents, many from abuse, and almost all their birth parents are not together.

By simply offering housing at a wage equivalent level will provide these types of young people on the streets the first step in the direction of a functional life existence not a feckless existence until they're dead or in jail.

Dis-loyal employers dishearten young staff

Listening constantly to stories of companies taking their operations across international borders to cut cost, has demonstrated lack of Made in America thinking. This prior pride factor gave great value to products, as well as the product makers. This part of our work ethic has been robbed from current generations of workers. Even if only in their own minds, employers are believed to no longer be loyal to the employee just the profit of the company.

Every time a phone is answered by customer support, and that call is handled by someone across the world, it sends a disloyalty message to the American caller. There becomes a disheartened thought process, seeing our jobs shipped abroad, and no way to be sure of job security.

Dis-enfranchised from Dreaming or Trying

The American dream? For me it was being self made. In recent years it has become the concept of home ownership exclusively. I am not sure where this concept originated, home ownership as the dreams totality. I was always under the impression that dreams belonged to the dreamer, not the media. If your dream was to start a business as I did, that was your American dream. If you got a job better than your father and were able to better support your family, for some that was their American dream. As I stated dreams should belong to the dreamer. By trying to make owning a house the American dream, now out of realistic attainment to most youth with current high housing prices vs. low wage, causes a entire segment of our population excluded from even trying to dream their own dream. We need to bring back American production and services back to America demonstrating to the youth of our society there we are offering security again.

Dis-illusioned to the idea of Security in Retirement From watching family and neighbors lose pensions and retirement accounts in the end of the last millennium and the first decade of this one, has further developed a belief of impossible. This is not the best for overall development of quality working generations in America.

Bring back the order to our Country's financial expectations within the working community.

The Domino Effect

Brand New Discoveries

4/23 – 5/2/17 while editing this manifesto.

As I wrote in the Denver Camping Urban Camping Ban chapter above. Early in December at a city council meeting, Councilman Espinoza requested that I reduce my thoughts on the "if only" factors to writing. As the dedication reads I also presented the pdf file to the Park Rangers. Ranger Dan as he is called took not only the time to read the 13 page proposal but took what he coined my manifesto to others : outreach, and people in power to effect change.

The fact is that from the 15th of December 2016 until April 2017 the area of the park where my street family sleeps was only disturbed once overnight. I had visited friends and the waterfront by us was scattered with random litter. I was the only one woken and I expressed apologies for the litter and noted my absence along with pointing out the 2 large empty trash bags outside my tent. I told them I would address it in daylight. I was responded to with an "OK, Thank You!"

It was not until late March that we were informed in writing that this camping area will be shut down and the curfew and structure laws would now be enforced as of April first. Both myself and one of my campmates that had read my proposal both said wow, the parks department took the proposal to heart. Now if only the City of Denver would look for a better way and stop this pettiness, attempting to disrupt houseless behavior and search to correct the root. This was e-mailed to all City Council at that time and I never received a single reply from any one of them including Rafael.

Fast forward to April third. We were told spring cleanup crew was scheduled to (sweep) pick up trash our area. We collected our trash and pick up litter up and down the adjacent sections of the park caused by normal discarded and blowing trash and bagged it all. Ready for the contractors and Park Rangers we disassembled our tents and left the area very clean. We were again told this area is no longer immune from citation and or police ticketing. This further supported either directly or clandestinely, behavior among Park Rangers had followed my proposal to the letter, providing us safety through the winter months.

Denver constantly pushes enforcement and Parks was now on the spot to eliminate the overnight sleepers in the park whether in clean areas or not. On the 12th of April I left with Max to tour Utah and Arizona sights. He was concerned for the Kaparowtis Plateau area of Grand Staircase Escalante, Utah proposed to be sold off for mining purposes due to "lack of anything of value to see up there" according to a State Representative. Max, being a photo journalist and valuing the view and being a Jeep enthusiast the 4 wheeling is pretty great too and would be a loss to the area if it were sold off. I returned flying in from Salt Lake City on the morning of the 22nd and camp was a total mess. Left behind tents and belongings, bikes and parts, excess clothing, etc. and I was more than pissed. Within days our biggest advocate Ranger Dan informed us once more to move elsewhere. He was coming in the morning with contractors to clean, it was the 29th of April almost a full month after the last cleanup. Again repeating this camping area was closed. Now keep in mind I have been told this was not a legal camping area since we started sleeping here in October of 2014, so the warnings comes with a grain of salt.

My family of 12 sleepers were prepared the prior night as we were the prior clean up which took less than 30 minutes including conversation with the Rangers. This day however our path was crossed by a dickhead attitude form Ranger #14, Willingham. At 4:10 am Ranger Hill woke us and delivered orders to be out by 8:00 and the crews would be stopping here first. This was the regular old jargon, we've heard time after time of the past 3 years. With 4 Rangers present outside my tent only Ranger Hill spoke, until he concluded, at which point Willingham felt it wise to interject "He's telling you the party is over." I lost my tongue and asked for his information right now. I continued with are you so stupid to think that any of these sleeping people looks to you like they are having a party. Having to listen to your asshole mouth, I wanted to say but kept it to myself. I did however commit to add him to the book I was working on. There is never an excuse for a Parks worker to belittle and inject personal and unprofessional opinions to people struggling on the streets being woken at 4:10 am. It is something that needs change hence this book, I pray it becomes a much needed eye opener.

This time even I gave up, I did not obey the order to be up and out at 8, nor did I get anyone else ready to go. That is my regular behavior but not a chance after I was spoken to in that manner at 4 am. This morning it didn't take 30 minutes for the contractors to move on, it took over an hour. And for conversation, it was not our normal happy interactions and helpful behavior. I took my sweet ass time and could not have cared less, they were welcome to ticket me. I wanted to get up and take pictures and video of us in action getting it cleaned and packed up.

It got to the point that Ranger Dan even got frustrated and acted out of character and said "you are all fucking pissing me off" others started to chime in to his frustrated conversation and I stopped them on a dime. He's allowed to express his being pissed off just as we do, and he is correct in this case. I basically figured if it was the last day and everyone was being evicted from the area then why bother rushing them. My attitude sucked, Ranger Dan's attitude was corrupted by the total vibe of everything the slowness and unprepared group and it all started with one dickhead attitude from Willingham. People need to treat people with respect regardless of personal attitude or belief. Professionals need to remain professional and we could have done a better job letting one dickheads attitude roll off our backs, mostly me.

All my campmates have relocated at this point, leaving me as the solo in that area. It makes me feel unsafe at times yet it is for certain always clean, lol.

Ranger Dan has now, at this point given me a ticket for having a structure in the park. My tent. It was in the afternoon and there was no good reason for my tent to be up at that point of the day other than being lazy and comfortable. I accepted the citation without argument. $100.00 is the fine for the first offense. The fines from there can increase for each additional if in same 12 months up to $999.00.

Since that ticket I had left my tent up for another week or two dropping it upon the arrival of the Rangers. At one point I was warned of the additional cost of the next ticket. For the benefits of myself and the Rangers being able to do their job without favoritism I had tried to sleep in just the sleeping bag. I was woken on several occasions and startled by rats and or geese walking over my sleeping bag. There is nothing restful in my mind sleeping outside a makeshift enclosure for some protection of self and belongings. Since then the roof of my tent has been sliced out and I realize now how good I had it. Last night a rat fell on my legs because if brought leftover chicken fingers back. I jumped to my feet in the sleeping bag, the rat was trapped inside for the second. I quickly unzipped the door and allowed him to escape. Before I was able to hear them chewing and stop them with a smack of the tent or growl.

Transient/ Urban Travelers

Train Hoppers the constant battle between Bulls and Bo's. Bulls being the rail police, Bo's being the hobos as termed by history.

I have met so many interesting people that travel through various parts of the country via freight trains. I never knew this segment of the population of Americans even existed in this century. Movies and the like, convey how often people just hop on a freight train headed in their direction. Yet as a normie I would never have conceived that this behavior was still prevalent in the 21st century. These individuals often carry dogs with them and use terms not understood on first pass. There are even guides to enter this as a lifestyle, both people and printed, neither shared without serious consideration. There are "hop out" mentors that will take on green freight hoppers, both offering physical protection as well as valuable information that will keep the new rider safer than venturing alone. I live directly under a BNSF yard on the South Platt River Trail, though no one hops here, many of them pass through and some have even camped with us. Freight Train Hoppers are true transients.

6 Figure Income Consultants

There is a growing understanding to cast the housing bills aside, among high demand and high paid consultants throughout the world. There is little reason to pay a year's worth of housing that is only occupied for 60 or so days in that year.

These consultants are mostly traveling and using the contract to provide sleeping accommodations while working the job, which is often several weeks if not months. When returning to whatever they consider their hometown they will opt to stay with friends, couch surfing or even get a hotel themselves. This person would likely never be described as transient yet they truly are. Most have a tie to somewhere they use as a permanent address for ID and mail.

Bikers/Hikers

In various cities I have traveled to as a tourist and when I lived in the Philadelphia area, I would run into individuals that were on adventures to hike or bike the country. Leaving behind the 9 to 5 and norm of working for food and housing, for a more challenging lifestyle of moving from place to place via bicycle or using standard transportation to arrive at the next location of their choosing to discover the outdoors.

These individuals for the time they are wandering would be considered transient.

Automobile Road Warriors

There is currently a phenomena in the US as well as Australia and other countries, where singles, families and small groups will venture out across the varied terrain in 4 wheel drive vehicles often with rooftop tents attached or living equip vehicles. They call it overlanding. Some do this all year round and others do it on summer break or other segments of the year. Those that overland year round with no permanent address are transients, yet the others often have a stable permanent address and are not, except while on the road.

Additionally there are those who choose to hit the open road in a mobile home or pop up camper living free of the traditional home. These folks are the new age transient. Some are even having fully equip club houses built on wheels to tow behind them, calling it tiny homes.

Aside – Any tiny homes that are stationary should be in no less than 3 story complexes, having a tiny home village is a waste of space for the overall concept of minimal impact. They should also have a no car clause, using bicycles and

184

car share instead. A bunch of club houses in one area where cars are larger than the home, is a waste. An apartment building with 3 or more stories and as many tiny units per floor as possible, units measuring no more than 150 square feet, this is an improvement in the community providing housing alternatives rather than more market priced condos or townhomes.

Transient as a "Code Word"

The gross misuse of the word transient among law enforcement needs to end. Law enforcement will utilize this word within a police report to deliver the Presiding Judge an indicator to raise bail or in fact revoke one's ability to be released on their own recognizance, assigning a status to unhoused individuals within their own community. Even when such movement from place to place does not exist whatsoever. This assignment is beyond inaccurate but also is very discriminatory in its use. When I was arrested in Denver, although having state ID issued a year prior, I was labeled the transient male, rather than the white male with dreadlocks and red hoodie as the original descriptions yielded.

This was unknown to me until reading the reports, at which time I understood perhaps why the Magistrate raised my bail after reading a report that spelled out the initial actor of any aggression was in fact the complainants, not myself. I enjoy court and rarely have had bench warrants issued for FTA. I was perplexed how any Judge reading the report would not wonder why I was being charged without the complainant also being charged when he was in fact the attacker and primary aggressor. My being transient, the officer not being able to correctly spell my name from my id to her report, the entirety of my group of 100 plus friends being described as the transient group, are all beyond inaccurate. But it sounds so much better to describe a transient male of the transient group, thus prolonging jail stays and degrading the individual via this description. The problem here in Denver is that they cannot get rid of us, so doesn't this by itself contradict the title "transient". YES!

Tent and sleeping bag residents that refuse to be exterminated or leave town <u>are not transient</u>.

The Smallest Percent
Druggies / Slobs / Zero Respect

It would seem that many of the people living indoors would like to simplify the issues connected to lacking a house. They try to group the majority into a category which they have actually invented, in their minds, to justify their denial of the root problems, "greedy dick heads".

The first category would be they are all just druggies! To suggest that "they are all" anything is a grand exaggeration and unrealistic. Those that are outside in locations where drugs are prevalent are surely at risk of becoming a product of the environment they now live. In cities where homelessness is being made illegal the speed drugs are a serious issue when being used just to stay awake during the night preventing police contact while sleeping, then crashing in daylight. As a means of curbing police contact but it without doubt happens anyway, because of the awake behaviors at 4 in the morning. The percentage of persons without housing is not far off the percentage of housed rich to poor persons who are on drugs or using booze or pharmaceutical to alter their state. Many of the people outside are sober and straight edge that I have met, all smoke weed to some degree, but just as many are using various drugs as a state altering device. By no means are all of those living on the streets there because they have drug problems exclusively or primarily.

Next are the normies that feel there is a large amount of mental problems with those living on the streets. This is an old image of the houseless in America and not the fact currently. Yes there are plenty of unbalanced folks on the streets but it is not the reason for most of those who are street dwellers from what I have seen in just under 3 years. I know more people indoors that have real mental issues then those I have interacted with on the streets daily.

Then next is a combined group of zero respect and slobs. This is actually my pet peeve from those on the streets. There is some level of relation to those who have lost their housing and loss of respect. Loss of respect for self, surroundings, and authority, but mostly stable richer people. I cannot pinpoint the relationship, but I can guess that there is some association to the reality of financial disarray within their lives which goes right along with being in disarray within their other facets of life. Poor at dealing with others, or cleaning up after one's self, having no respect for self and surroundings seems to go hand in hand, across the board with many that live on the streets.

The rare, is the individual that is excessively neat and always attempts to stay invisible leaving no trace, can hang with me. Street slobs are a larger percentage in my experience than those who have residential junk yard properties or hording houses. I blame part on overall lack of supervision while growing up, preventing the behaviors being pounded in their heads from a young age. No doubt those on the street feel they don't have to impress anyone or do anymore for their community than their community does for them.

This is another of the domino effect factors, lack of understanding from others and overall behavior education (poor programming) leads to a full circle of low respect. There are plenty of the normies that are litter bugs themselves, but a much larger percentage of those on the streets leave mess behind. In some cases it is because they are being run out of the space

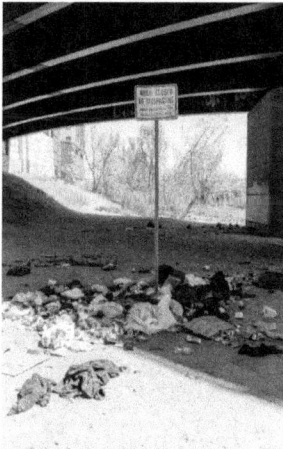

they were occupying in public and expected to leave in a hurry so only important items are packed and carried.

Even my camping area gets out of control sometimes if I am visiting elsewhere for a few consecutive days, leaving the campers to their own without me cleaning up, every day. I am the only person beside a few loners that pick up after others.

Most of the people that I allow to invade my zen space do their best to respect me enough to control their litter. However other areas in the park and city are left to the individuals who usually refuse to pick up after others. They exhibit a bad attitude for their surroundings and the area in which they sleep. I am not sure where I crossed into the OCD for the park to be clean, but it is about the largest difference between my area and others.

Often the police will run names of those in a camping

area and sometimes get an outstanding warrant on someone. Once they arrest the person and place them in the patrol vehicle they don't inform the rest of the people in the camp area that they knew to bring trash bags. Provide them bags and sit with the person arrested, cuffed in the back seat, waiting until all trash is removed from sight. But no they just take one or two from the camp, leaving their property and mess along with the mess of the others. After the officers leave, in most cases the rest of the camp packs wanted property and leave to a new area because the houseless assume that the police will be back to hassle them and their friends again. This causes an empty area with a ton of trash left behind costing the city thousands of dollars for contractors to come in and remove it at a later time. And that often takes weeks.

There is however in my mind a simple way to correct the slob and disrespectful portion of the street dwellers. *Just fucking have police issue littering tickets without hesitation.*

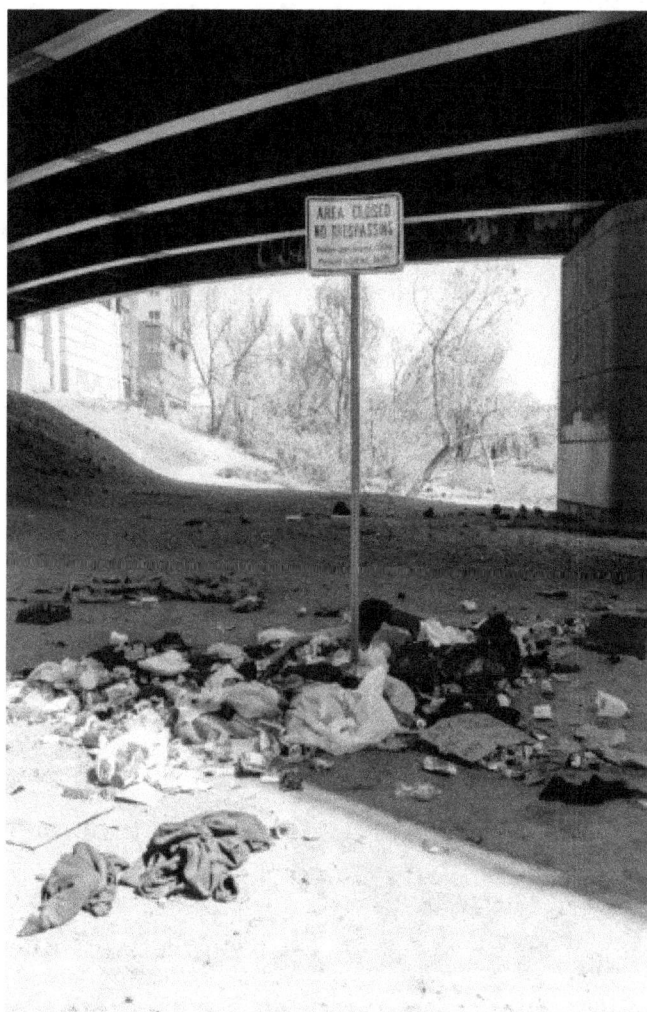

Background: how this started

As witnessed by 100 of our friends, and as I recall the events the following week when I had clarity to write them down.

It was a beautiful October First Friday, I intended to spend the evening strolling The Art Walk on Santa Fe Drive in Downtown Denver, where I had spent most First Fridays since relocating to Denver the previous September. I'm a full time writer is working on various book projects; additionally have a passion for being a temporary human canvas for professional body painters. I was playing tour guide to a former roommate of my two sons from Boca Raton, Florida a college student in

Denver visiting family. Daniela and I were looking forward to joining up with others including her cousin, and have a great evening of art and local food.

The evening however took a very "shitty" detour to include my first tour inside the walls of the Denver City Jail.

A then random woman refused to pick up her dogs poop in Commons Park in violation of 39.15 - (D) of the City Code. First, I had to excuse myself from my party to check that my eyes saw correctly. Did Nicole

DeJohn's big brown pup, in fact poop on the grass and Nicole just walk away? I saw correctly and let her now 20 yards away to clean up her dog's shit. She replied "I will! When your pick up your trash."

What Nicole DeJohn was referring to, was the cumulative park litter, which has always been a tremendously unchecked problem in the areas of

Commons park where the "stoners" congregate most every day. Since the recreational Marijuana legalization, Commons Park and the Scenic Hill at 16th and The Platt River has earned GOOGLE ranking as "Stoner Hill", even Denver's Boys in Blue use the colloquial title. DeJohn and newlywed husband Doug W White had previously made a stink about the litter. A week earlier in late September 2015, addressing a local charity known for supporting the youth within the park, expressing disdain for the group of stoner friends.

At the beginning of summer Parks executive Scott Gilmore along with Police and Park Rangers had discussed trash concerns with me, as a regular fixture at Stoner Hill and involved on both sides of the issues. I suggested additional trash receptacle, which Gilmore had delivered to the area the same afternoon, as well as opening the water fountain and bathrooms over the next 2 days. Progress and considerable reduction in litter thanks to my understanding the needs of the group to help find solutions and Gilmore's willingness to listen. The Stoner group at large was clearly instructed by Authorities to enforce and promote litter control within the Park.

Anyone that knows me personally knows that I don't condone mess in my area, and this pup pooped 5 yards from my bike and backpack, causing me to address the issue.

It seems, Nicole DeJohn arrived home complaining to her newlywed husband Doug W White that I had according to White, followed her home, once he came and found the red shirt dreadlocks guy about 5'9" in the park as his 911 call demonstrates after he returned home.

This rather large guy comes and points me out of the group of 100, asking me, who followed his wife? I asked what he was talking about? With the brown dog he stated with anger and aggressiveness in his tone, finger pointing, and body language. His behavior was enough to cause others to pay attention to this man's next move and be alert and on guard. Standing 6 ft or better this guy was clearly being intimidating. I let him know no one had followed his wife and I personally had addressed the "dog shit", but he can come and clean up now, he refused.

My legal opinion, Mr. White violated 18-3.206 Menacing under Colorado State Law, as well as refusal to clean up 39-15 (d) and for certain disturbing the Peace of over 50 individuals.

1) Woman refuses to remove her dog's excrement breaking the law.

2) Nicole DeJohn returns home and exacerbates what she already knows to be a hot button for her newlywed husband.

3) Husband Doug W White summarily leaves the home to confront me in the park.

4) White refuses my request to retrieve his dogs poop?

5) White's intentions leaving his home are seemingly criminal, exacerbated by his disdain for my associated friends.

6) White disrupts group peacefully enjoying the park.

7) Threatens to shoot any individuals approaching his address on 911 tapes

8) Makes false accusations against me.

9) White and DeJohn are not charged by police, yet I am, for making threats and disturbing the peace. Both Dismissed, due to their FTA.

Sidenote – If I were the Denver judge behind the bench on this case, I would have told that prosecutor he had 2 hours to get the witnesses into the courtroom or they and he would be held in contempt just for tying up Mr Jackson for the past 3 months and wasting the time of the court and its staff. If you can't, don't come back into my courtroom again and find another job! He had stated that the victim had moved and would like to put this behind them. *That is not his or their call, it is playing the system. They moved 5 minutes away.*

Denver Picked On The Wrong Group

[It wasn't me, but it could have been.]

From what I see, this was a tactic to remove the houseless from the park, not provide additional safety to the other park users. NO LAW CAN BE TESTED WITHOUT FIRST TICKETING AND THEN FIGHTING.

In the middle of October 2016, just before my 50th birthday, my room-mates came home and were upset because some of our friends had been ticketed and told they were not able to return to Stoner Hill (Commons Park Denver) for the next 90 days.

I was genuinely confused!

I compelled them to stop, and let me see if I am following the story correctly.

ME- So you're telling me that Peanut and Troy both got caught with a joint in the Park... and they were issued tickets by Denver Police?

THEM-Yup!

ME- ok then after ticketing them the officer wrote them a separate piece of paper telling them they were banned from that Park property for 90 Days.

THEM- Yup!

ME- ok, that's way fucked up, because the law has a defined penalty for that behavior, in a Denver Park. And when did Sgt become a judge to issue sentencing without oversight or a hearing?

So I looked into this matter over the next week. I connected with Park Rangers who are not able to issue the ban and Denver Police Officers that work in the area of Stoner Hill.

I looked up the Park Directive and how it came to be. Printing it and displaying it to Officers that know me. Asking, HOW??? Those surveyed were split on this issue, some agreeing, others (the ticket writers) supporting and asking me why I would choose to stand up defending those issued Park Suspensions. Asking how much I really knew about the ones ticketed. I would reply "I don't care if they just shot someone, sexually assaulted them and dumped them in the river, it has nothing to do with this suspension for a marijuana joint."

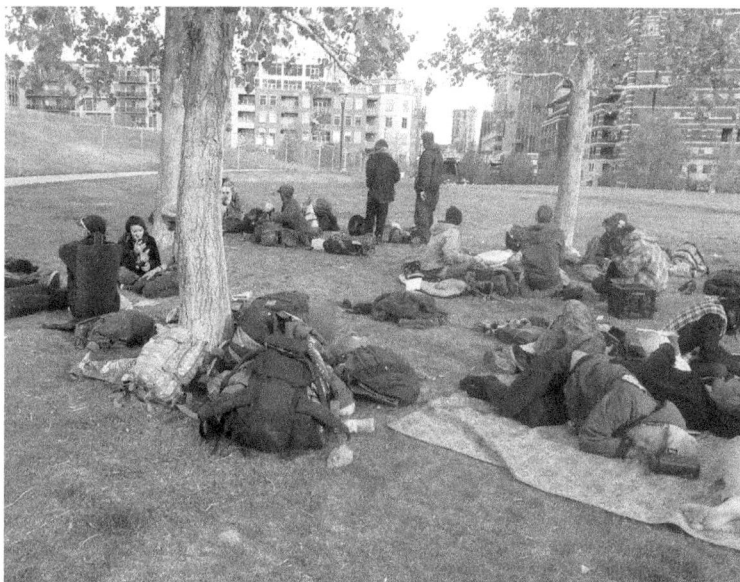

(sic. Denver Park Directive 2016-1)
• Illegal Drugs: Controlled substances, as defined and regulated under the Uniform Controlled Substances Act of 2013, as codified and amended in Article ~8 of Title 18 of the Colorado Revised Statutes. This includes (1) Schedule 1 controlled substances, and (2) Schedule II, III, IV and V controlled substances not legally in a person's possession.
• Illegal Drug-Related Activity: The act of distributing, transferring, selling, sharing, baying, consuming, using, or illegally possessing Illegal Drugs.
1. Purpose: The purpose of this Directive 2016-1 - is to address serious and chronic public health and safety problems caused by illegal drug-related activity in City Parks and the Cherry Creek Greenway. There

have been persistent and increasing complaints from park patrons, trail users, law enforcement, Parks and Public Works staff, and other members of the public about misconduct and threatening conduct associated with drug selling, drug buying and drug use in City Parks and in and along the Cherry Creek Greenway. These problems include assaults, shootings, and other acts of violence or threats of violence, used needles and other drug paraphernalia, people passed out or incapacitated due to drug use, vandalism, activities of drug sellers, drug buyers and drug users in and about the Cherry Creek Greenway that obstruct passage or make for unsafe passage of pedestrians, joggers, skaters and bicyclists on the Cherry Creek Trail, and other misbehavior that intimidates and frightens members of the public and has resulted in making the City Parks and the Cherry Creek Greenway a much less attractive place for the public to recreate and enjoy nature and the outdoors. This Directive 2016-1 is necessary to reduce or eliminate the problems and hazards of illegal drug-related activity in City Parks and the Cherry Creek Greenway.

2. Directive: The following Directive, as issued by the Executive Director of the Department of Parks and Recreation ("DPR Director"), shall be applicable at all times in the City Parks and in the Cherry Creek Greenway, as said Greenway is defined in the Parks-Public Works MOU, i.e., from Confluence Park to Downing Street and including the entire area within the floodwalls as well as the sidewalks, landscaped areas and other infrastructure outside of the floodwalls from interior curb to interior curb along

Speer Boulevard (the "Cherry Creek Greenway ").
Duration: Directive 2016-1 shall be in effect from
September 1, 2016, through February 26, 2017
("Duration "), subject to any time extension specified
below in this Directive.

So for the rest of the Country - yet to recreationally
legalize marijuana, may read this and find no
problem with the association of Scheduled Drugs to
include marijuana. However, I left New Jersey two
and a half years ago, so I could not get more than a
$150.00 ticket with no criminal implications for
wrongful use or display of marijuana. To me this was
the manner in which marijuana should be treated;
and I believed this from about the age of 18, when I
realized how untrue the educational system
portrayed the consumption of marijuana.

So how was it possible here in Denver Colorado
where the State as a whole legalized the product for
recreational use by people over 21, Amendment 64 of
the State Constitution. The friends they were
discussing were both over 21, therefore in possession

of the marijuana 100% legally likely with high taxes paid on the product itself.

So this discovery from my further investigations prompted me to take action. I began with a letter to the local papers, and the ACLU to give my opinion of the stupidity surrounding these 90 day Park suspensions.

From: echoman503@yahoo.com (Jackson)
To:intake@aclu-co.org
10/30/16 at 11:17 PM

FREEDOM OF MOVEMENT -Free Our Parks and Indigent

In my opinion, Denver City and Denver City Parks Department with assistance from Police is making a huge mistake. I say this because I see a clear violation of both double jeopardy, as well freedoms of movement both Constitutionally Protected Rights. By setting standards for Parks Directive so low that Americans of Denver are establishing a Dictatorship / Martial Law or at least the three Parks executives are doing so. Removing access to Community, as well as resources, both to dislocated people without electronics and Outreach Units themselves that use public parks for access points for humanitarian measures.

At no point would I be prevented from using a street because I was given a speeding violation, I would pay or fight the ticket. No person should be put into a position of receiving additional trespass citations for a minor infraction of their protected right to recreational marijuana without a hearing.

If cited for weed which carries no penalty beyond what the laws of Colorado allow, further area restriction is wrong. Smoking a joint of marijuana when of age where no probation oversight exists upon the accused, imposing additional penalties beyond established laws of the State, it becomes cruel and unusual punishment. If a dog is off leash during an unregulated time where the owner is cited almost equally under law as smoking a joint, will they be told to remove themselves for 90 days from the Park for improper use?

With specifics and regarding Stoner Hill / Commons Park the error uncorrected will create a twofold problem: such a vacuum, based on almost 3 years direct knowledge of the drug community in Downtown Denver and 20 owning a pizza place, becomes a gigantic flaw. To leave such a well policed THC Park to illegally unleashed dogs who's homeowner/ guardians are irresponsible in cleaning up their dogs' excrement, and of course the narcotics and roofless users will have zero hindrance; as well as the crowd relocating costing additional acrimony to the community in whole.

Background: Hello, my name is Jackson, many who have read this far have see me at Stoner Hill spending lazy days, yet I am 50 years old and have 2 adult children finishing College in Florida. I lived much of my life as a businessman turning millions in sales, as most Denverites hate, I came because marijuana became legal. In 2014 I arrived in Denver and have become a sort of Caretaker at Commons Park and my section of the Platt River. I fear that effort for improvement in the past 2 years will become futile if this illegal restriction of Americans from Public Spaces continues.

To: Mark Silverstein, Legal Director ACLU COLORADO

Mark I currently am aware of a 23yr old young man who has not only been ticketed for smoking a joint in Commons Park, area included in the Cherry Creek Directive from Parks but, also banned for 90 days. In my opinion and I believe you concur, this is a clear act of continued entrapment for the trespass violation. He has additionally received his written trespass ticket as I witnessed 3 weeks ago. I heard the officer tell him if he is present in the park again he would arrest him. I found this to be beyond bizarre!

Please contact me back if you think this is up your alley. I will have him get arrested if need be by being present in the park with me doing nothing illegal or disruptive. Thanks You any Consideration. — with Troy Holm at Stoner Hill - Downtown Denver.

Response came from the ACLU and none of the papers I had provided with the same email.

I shortly after met with the ACLU-CO attorney's and discussed them taking the case for one of my friends. Attached is excerpt of the Motion that the ACLU prepared and we are waiting until the 22nd of February to determine the Judge's ruling on the Motion to Dismiss.

One way or the other, I am old enough to realize the political climate of Judicial err, knowing there are times, being the Judge to oppose local law enforcement becomes an overpowering reason to err. Providing the ability to Appeal their ruling.

I am quite sure the ACLU will do just that if the ruling does not come back in favor of my friend Troy.

Update: Feb 22 2017 – Denver Judge Rules Park Ban Unconstitutional. It was a slam dunk, but I did giggle that the Judge was unwilling to discuss the ruling on the motion in open court. Providing a written ruling and quickly and quietly dismissing the case against Troy.

This protects the court from having the audio requested by news agencies as well as grandstanding by the winning side for the same reasons of the audio becoming news worthy. With a written ruling it is what it is and little is left for either side to play off of for public relations purposes.

Below is the ACLU motion and the Judge's ruling from the county court of Denver.

Update March 15, I was told by the ACLU that the city of Denver will be appealing the judge's ruling on this motion, rather than just admit wrongdoing and adjust the ban to allow for not guilty plea, preventing the lack of due process.

Denver County, Colorado 1437 Bannock Street Denver, CO 80202	
THE CITY AND COUNTY OF DENVER, **PLAINTIFF** v. **HOLM, TROY DANIEL** **DEFENDANT**	

Attorney or Party Without Attorney (Name and Address):	Case Number:
	16GS013978
Phone Number: E-mail:	
FAX Number: Atty. Reg. #:	Division 3F Courtroom

ORDER re: DEFENDANT'S MOTION TO DISMISS

This matter comes before the court on the Defendant's Motion to Dismiss. Defendant Holm was charged with two counts for alleged violations of the Denver Revised Municipal Code ("D.R.M.C.") as follows: D.R.M.C 39-4 Restriction or Prohibition of Uses and Activities; and 38-115 Trespass. The statutes read as follows:

- **Sec. 39-4. - Restriction or prohibition of uses and activities.**

  (a) It shall be unlawful for any person, other than authorized personnel, to engage in any use of or activities in any area or part of any park, parkway, mountain park, or other recreational facility in violation of any temporary directive issued by the manager restricting or prohibiting such use or activities.

  (b) It shall be unlawful for any person, other than authorized personnel, to engage in any team sport activities, as defined in adopted rules, in violation of any rules or public notice restricting or prohibiting such team sport activities in any passive recreation use area, as defined in adopted rules.

  (Ord. No. 446-12, § 1, 9-10-12; Ord. No. 728-15, § 1, 11-9-15)

- **Sec. 38-115. - Trespass.**

  (a) It is unlawful for any person knowingly to enter or remain upon the premises of another when consent to enter or remain is absent, denied, or withdrawn by the owner, occupant, or person having lawful control thereof.

  (b) It shall be prima facie evidence that consent is absent, denied, or withdrawn, to enter or remain upon the premises of another when:

  (1) Any person fails or refuses to remove himself from said premises when requested to leave by the owner, occupant or person having lawful control thereof; or

213

(2) Such premises are fenced or otherwise enclosed in a manner designed to exclude intruders; or

(3) Private property or public property, which is not then open to the public, is posted with signs which give notice that entrance is forbidden.

* * *

At the center of both charges is Temporary Directive 2016-1: "Suspension of Right to Access of Parties Engaged in Drug-Related Activity from City Parks and the Cherry Creek Greenway" , a temporary directive issued by the Director of Parks and Recreation which purportedly is effective from September 1, 2016 - February 26, 2017. This directive suspends the right of a person "engaged in Illegal Drug-Related Activity" from accessing or using the City Parks and the Cherry Creek Greenway in which the Illegal Drug-Related Activity occurred for a period of ninety (90) days. A full rendition of Temporary Directive 2016-1 is incorporated into this Order as Apendix A, for consideration upon appeal. However, discussion of several aspects of Temporary Directive 2016-1 are discussed below.

According to the directive, "Illegal Drug-Related Activity" is defined as "[t]he act of distributing, transferring, selling, sharing, buying, consuming, using, or illegally possessing Illegal Drugs." Specifically, and of most interest to this court, is the enforcement provision of the Temporary Directive which reads as follows:

> Enforcement: If a Denver Police Officer should determine that a person has committed a Violation, the Denver Police Officer may issue a notice to said violator suspending the right of the violator (the "Suspension Notice") from accessing or using City Parks or the Cherry Creek Greenway, depending on the location(s) of the Violation, for a period of ninety (90) days *from the date of the Suspension Notice. The Suspension shall be immediately in effect upon the issuance of the Suspension Notice.* Failure to comply with the Suspension Notice during the 90-day Suspension shall be grounds for issuance of a ticket and assessment of a penalty as provided in section 1-13, DRMC. The person subject to the Suspension Notice need not be charged, tried or convicted of any crime, infraction, or administrative citation in order for the Suspension Notice to be issued or effective. *(emphasis added)*

The Temporary Directive then dictates a fairly elaborate administrative appeals process, whereby a person who receives a Suspension Notice has ten days to file an appeal with the Department of Parks and Recreation Director. Once the appeal is filed, a hearing "shall be scheduled for a date no later than twelve (12) calendar days following the date the Appeal is filed". After this hearing is scheduled, notice of the hearing must be sent to the party no later than four days following the date the date that the appeal is filed. The Administrative Hearing Officer (appointed by the Department of Parks and Recreation Director) may continue the hearing for up to 10 days upon request of either the suspended party or the City, in order for additional witnesses and evidence to be presented, and provides that "[t]he Suspension Notice shall remain in effect during this continuance."

2

214

In fact, by the very terms of Temporary Directive 2016-1, the Suspension Notice remains in effect from the moment that a Denver Police Officer "determines that a person has committed a Violation" (by what standard the directive is silent), hands an alleged violator the Suspension Notice, continuing throughout the administrative appeal process, and further continues unless and until the Administrative Hearing Officer "reverses the Suspension Notice". In order to acquire a reversal, the Administrative Hearing Officer must find that the alleged violator has proven that either the violator did not commit the violation, that the Suspension Notice was not legally issued, or was issued "in violation of other law".

After the hearing is completed, as per the terms of the Temporary Directive, the Administrative Hearing Officer has an additional five days to issue a written decision. This means that from the time a person is immediately banned from a public park upon issuance of a Suspension Notice, and even assuming that the alleged violator does not wait the ten days to request a hearing, to the conclusion of the hearing challenging the issuance, twenty-seven days may pass before a wrongly inflicted "violator" receives reprieve. If the alleged violator takes the 10 days given to initiate the challenge, thirty-seven days may pass. All the while, the alleged violator has been deprived access to a public park or area, and is subjected to criminal charges should the subject present himself at the noted public location. This is a substantial proportion of the 90 day suspension period.

There is, by the very wording of Temporary Directive 2016-1, no pre-deprivation due process afforded to a person who is subjected to a Suspension Notice. The Temporary Directive is meticulously crafted in this way, while asserting no compelling reason to support such a pre-deprivation approach, nor does this court find that such a compelling reason to deny procedural Due Process in this way has been established by the City. The infringement upon the right to utilize a public area could easily be delayed until the administrative hearing has been held, the alleged violator has had a meaningful opportunity to be heard, and the hearing officer has made a written determination as to the basis of the deprivation. Essentially, the exact procedures mandated by Temporary Directive 2016-1 could be implemented, but the sanction of banishment from public parks could be imposed after procedural Due Process has been afforded. Instead, deprivation of the liberty to utilize a public space is immediately imposed upon the ambiguous "determination" ("ambiguous" because no standards for determination are noted - for example, requiring the sanctioning officer to witness firsthand the alleged violation, or with any indication regarding the standard of proof the officer must assert to support such determination) by an officer that a violation has occurred.

The court must weigh three factors to determine whether the action of the City in this case has deprived a person of a liberty interest without due process of law as follows: 1) the private interest that will be affected by the official action; 2) the risk of an erroneous deprivation of such interest through the procedures used, and 3) the City's interest, including the function involved and the administrative burdens that the additional requirement would entail. Matthews v. Eldridge, 424 U.S. 319, 336 (1976); Van Sickle v. Boyes, 797 P.2d 1267 (Colo.1990).

The interest of the City in this case is recognized as the need to rid the parks of persons who utilize the area as a sanctuary for drug use. This is seen as a legitimate state/city interest. The court also recognizes a private interest of a member of the public to have access to public parklands, as recognizes the same as a liberty interest. Further, the risk of an erroneous deprivation of the liberty

3

interest in using public land is great under Temporary Directive 2016-1, as the "determination" is made by an officer without standards imposed, allowing for unfettered, unchecked discretion on the part of an officer. Finally, considering the City's interest and the relative ease at which the procedures could be changed (essentially imposing very little difference in cost and time upon the City) the deprivation of the liberty interest is found to be offensive to a *Matthews* analysis. As the park suspensions under Temporary Directive 2016-1 take effect immediately, within the pure unchecked discretion of any police officer on the scene, and with a complete lack of any pre-deprivation Due Process, the suspensions violate procedural Due Process protections, and are found unconstitutional for this reason.

As the two counts charged against the Defendant in this case are wholly reliant upon the validity of Temporary Directive 2016-1, the Defendant's motion is GRANTED.

SO ORDERED,

_____   _2/22/17_____
Judge Clarisse Gonzales   Date
Denver County Court

Certificate of Service

The undersigned hereby certifies that a true and accurate copy of the foregoing Order re: was delivered to the following parties, U.S. postage prepaid, on the __22_____ of __February_____, 2017.

Hand Delivered in Open Court.

_____
Linda Baltazar, Clerk to Judge C. Gonzales

4

216

III. The Effect of the Parks Exclusion on Mr. Holm

22. Commons Park is extremely important to Mr. Holm. First and foremost, Commons Park is Mr. Holm's chief source of community. Mr. Holm, like many of the people who often spend their days in Commons Park, is houseless. Commons Park represents a gathering point for Mr. Holm and his community – a place to spend time with friends who have become his only family. Depriving Mr. Holm of this community effectively uproots Mr. Holm from a central feature of his familial life.

Pic added for manifesto only

23. Additionally, because houseless people are known to congregate around Commons Park, the park represents a key locus for the distribution of food and services to houseless people. For example, for the past two years, the group 180 Outreach regularly comes to

Commons Park to distribute snacks, toiletries, and warm clothing to the houseless community. Stand Up For Kids also uses Commons Park as a key location for dispensing services; they give out clothes, warm coats, good food, and gifts around the holidays.

pics added for manifesto only

Similarly, a wonderful man named Dale Swan and his two children regularly bring beverages and snacks to

the Commons Park houseless community. By banning Mr. Holm from Commons Park, Denver has taken away a key means for Mr. Holm to get warm clothing, warm food, and community.

ARGUMENT

I. Directive 2016-1 is void

and unenforceable because the Department of Parks and Recreation did not have the legal authority to issue it. A. The Department of Parks and Recreation can only issue a directive if Denver law explicitly grants the Department the power to do so. 24. "No matter how important, conspicuous, and controversial the issue, and regardless of how likely the public is to hold the Executive Branch politically accountable, an administrative agency's power to regulate in the public interest must always be grounded in a valid grant of authority." FDA v. Brown & Williamson Tobacco Corp., 529 U.S. 120, 161 (2000). 25. This fundamental principle is enshrined in both Colorado and Denver law. In Colorado, "No rule shall be issued except within the power delegated to the agency and as authorized by law." C.R.S. § 24-2-103(8)(a). In Denver, "No officer, employee, agent or agency, board or commission or member thereof of the city shall have power or authority to adopt any rules or regulations save and except by and under the authority of the Charter or ordinances of the city." DRMC § 2-92. 26. Any rule that is promulgated without statutory authority is void and unenforceable. DRMC § 2-99(1) ("Rules and regulations shall not be enforced unless they are adopted pursuant to [the DRMC]"); see also 5 U.S.C. § 706(2)(C) ("The reviewing court shall . . . hold unlawful and set aside agency action, findings, and conclusions found to be . . . in excess of statutory jurisdiction, authority, or limitations, or short of statutory right."); C.R.S. § 24-4-103(8)(a). 27. Under black letter law, the Executive Director of the

Department of Parks and Recreation can only issue a directive if the power to do so has been explicitly delegated to her under law. C.R.S. § 24-2-103(8)(a); DRMC § 2-92. If the Director issues a directive that is not authorized by law, it is void and unenforceable. DRMC § 2-99(1). B. Denver law does not grant the Department of Parks and Recreation the power to ban people from public parks. 28. While the Director of the Parks Department has the right to manage, operate, and control the parks by prohibiting certain activities in the parks including the use of illegal drugs, nothing in Denver law provides the Director with the authority to prohibit certain people from entering the parks. To the contrary, Denver law explicitly withholds that power from the Department. Id. 6 29. The Department of Parks and Recreation is entrusted with the "management, operation, and control" of Denver parks. DRMC § 2.4.4. To carry this out, the Department is authorized to: Adopt rules and regulations for the management, operation and control of parks, parkways, mountain parks and other recreational facilities, and for the use and occupancy, management, control, operation, care, repairing and maintenance of all structures and facilities thereon, and all land on which the same are located and operated. DRMC § 39-1 (emphasis added). 30. Under DRMC § 39-1, the Department has one set of powers to regulate parks, and different set of powers to regulate the structures and facilities that exist in parks. The Department has the authority to adopt rules and regulations for the "occupancy" of facilities within parks. Id. However, under the plain language of Denver law, the Department does not have the power to adopt regulations for the "occupancy" of the parks themselves – only the structures and facilities. Id. 31. Directive 2016-1 regulates the "occupancy" of a park, not of a facility within a park. The Directive therefore exceeds the Department's statutory grant of authority under DRMC § 39-1. 32. This was a sagacious choice by Denver legislators. Had Denver chosen to give the Department this authority, the grant would have been unconstitutional, inevitably embroiling the City in costly litigation. See parts II and III, infra. 33. The Department cannot resort to statutory interpretation to save its illegal regulation. It is a "well-established statutory construction rule that words omitted by the Legislature may not be supplied as a means of interpreting a statute." Miller v. City & Cnty. of Denver, 2013 COA 78, ¶ 21. To the contrary, "If the plain language of a statute is unambiguous and clear, we need not employ other tools of statutory interpretation." Colo. Dep't of Corr. v. Madison, 85 P.3d 542, 547 (Colo. 2004). Here, the plain language of the statute is clear – the Department has the authority to regulate the occupancy of facilities within the parks, but not the occupancy of the parks themselves. No amount of legal gymnastics can change the fact that Denver law does not give the Department the authority to promulgate 2016-1. 34. Furthermore, "Where [the legislature] includes particular language in one section of a statute but omits it in another section of the same Act, it is generally presumed that [the legislature] acts intentionally and purposely in the disparate inclusion or exclusion." Gozlon-Peretz v. United States, 498 U.S. 395, 404 (1991). 35. Because Directive 2016-1 was promulgated without authority, it is void and unenforceable. DRMC § 2-99(1). As a result, Mr. Holm was not in violation of any valid order on October 17 when he was present in Commons Park. 7 II. Directive 2016-1 violates the United States Constitution's guarantee of procedural due process. A. Mr. Holm has a constitutionally-protected liberty interest in being in Commons Park. 36. It is beyond dispute that enforcement of Directive 2016-1, i.e. the issuance of suspension notices, implicates park-goers' constitutionally- protected liberty interest "to be in parks or on other city lands of their choosing that are open to the public generally." Catron v. City of St. Petersburg, 658 F.3d 1260, 1266 (11th Cir. 2011) (citing City of Chicago v. Morales, 527 U.S. 41, 53-54 (1999)). 37. According to the United States Supreme Court: We have expressly identified [the] right to remove from one place to another according to inclination as an attribute of personal liberty protected by the Constitution. Indeed, it is apparent that an individual's decision to remain in a public place of his choice is as much a part of his liberty as the freedom of movement inside frontiers that is a part of our heritage. City of Chicago v. Morales, 527 U.S. 41, 53-54 (1999) (internal citations and quotations omitted). 38. This liberty interest dates to the founding of the country, and has been recognized for more than a century. As the Supreme Court declared in 1900, "the right of locomotion, the right to remove from one place to another according to inclination, is an attribute of personal liberty." Williams v. Fears, 179 U.S. 270, 274 (1900). 39. This liberty interest has been recognized by courts across the country. See, e.g., Vincent v. City of Sulphur, 805 F.3d 543, 548 (5th Cir. 2015) ("Supreme Court decisions amply support the proposition that there is a general right to go to or remain on public property for lawful purposes."); Kennedy v. City Of Cincinnati, 595 F.3d 327, 337 (6th Cir. 2010) (recognizing that man excluded from a public pool had a "clearly established right to remain on public property."); Johnson, 310 F.3d at 495 (holding "that the Constitution protects a right to travel locally through public spaces and roadways."); City of New York v. Andrews, 186 Misc. 2d 533, 545 (N.Y. Sup. Ct. 2000) ("The Federal Constitution . . . protects a person's right to remain in the public area of his or her choice, and to loiter there for innocent purposes, according to inclination."); Yeakle v. City of Portland, 322 F. Supp. 2d 1119 (D. Or. 2004); Catron v. City of St. Petersburg, 658 F.3d 1260 (11th Cir. 2011). B. Under the federal and state constitutional guarantees of procedural due process, a person cannot be deprived of a liberty interest unless the person is first given notice of the potential deprivation and an opportunity for a hearing. 40. The United States and Colorado Constitutions both bar state actors from depriving a person of a liberty interest without due process of law. U.S. Const. amend. XIV; Colo. Cont. art. II, § 25. 41. Under both the Colorado and United States Constitutions, to evaluate whether a state actor has deprived a person of a liberty interest without due process of law, this court must weigh three factors: (1) the "private interest that will be affected by the official action," (2) "the risk of an erroneous deprivation of such interest through the procedures used," and (3) "the Government's

The above is a short excerpt from the ACLU's 14 pg Motion demonstrating with only my common sense beliefs of Constitutional Rights, I was not off target of the ACLU and other legal professionals.

Aside - And further my belief that only 17 camping tickets issued with over 8500 contacts by DPD, is because they do not want to take the risk of running across someone like me, that will take it to the higher courts.

www.ingramcontent.com/pod-product-compliance
Lightning Source LLC
LaVergne TN
LVHW051047080426
835508LV00019B/1755